TRUE LOVE

TRUE LOVE

How to Make Your Relationship Sweeter, Deeper and More Passionate

DAPHNE ROSE KINGMA

CONARI PRESS

Cover Photography: © PhotoDisc, Inc.
Cover and Book Design: Suzanne Albertson

Library of Congress Cataloging-in-Publication Data available upon request.
ISBN 1-57324-863-0
LCC #90-84636

Printed in Canada

02 03 04 05   TC   10 9 8 7 6 5 4 3 2 1

For Dominique
whose true vocation is to love

*None of these words would ever have been
delivered to the page without the loving encouragement
and indefatigable effort of my editor-of-genius,
Mary Jane Ryan, to whom I offer
a garland of boundless thanks.*

TRUE LOVE

Cherishing Your Beloved

Treasuring Your Relationship

THE TRANSFORMATIONS OF LOVE

This little book is a prescription for true love: love that lasts, love that heals, love that transforms, love that brings inestimable joy. While there are many books that discuss the hidden psychological agendas in relationships and offer a variety of coping mechanisms, this in not my purpose here. Rather, I offer this book as a gift of nurturance and mending for your love, a course for encouraging the skills of loving. No matter who you are, you can enhance your relationship by incorporating these attitudes and behaviors.

You can read it from cover to cover or open it at random and read an entry a day. One particularly valuable way to use it is to pick an item and ask your mate to try to do that thing—for the day, for a week, for a month—while he or she does the same for you. Chances are you'll both pick things you really need and getting what you want will greatly enhance the love between you.

Love flourishes only when we have psychologically prepared ourselves for it. Part I, *The Conditions of Love,* talks about this preparation, offering some of the knowings we must have in order to create a felicitous climate for love. These include insights that will change the way you view your relationship, what is possible in it, and the expectations you have for it. Part II, *The Practices of Love,* offers suggestions for gestures and actions which, if consciously performed, will insure that the love you have planted will flourish and grow. It is divided into three sections: "Nourishing Your Loving Self," "Cherishing Your Beloved," and "Treasuring Your Relationship," because true love consists of taking care of yourself, the other person, and the relationship itself.

Finally, true love has a very high purpose. It is to deliver us—through the mirroring presence of the person who loves us—to the deepest reaches of our selves, to a sense of the meaning of our lives and to a fulfillment of that purpose. Part III, *The Transformations of Love,* provides some ways to call upon the power of love to recast us into who we truly can be. This is the highest grace of love, its truest calling and its greatest work. It is in this capacity to love that we truly have the power to move mountains and to change the world.

In each of us there is a tremendous longing for love. The love we desire is not only the euphoric butterflies-in-the-stomach feeling of new romance, but also the ineffable consolation of being deeply known, received, and cared for, the profound sense of peace and security of spirit that comes from being deeply connected to another human being.

Achieving the first is often easy. Romantic love rides in on a wave of impulse or attraction, kindled by moonlight, the magic of music, the spell-binding fragrance of soft summer evenings. The second—true love—is much more difficult. All too often the loves we fall into disappoint us. We want to sustain the delectable feelings but we can't. We want to enhance and deepen the bonds between us but we don't know how.

I began to write this book after many years of working with people whose deepest hearts' desire was to feel the joy and companionship of real love. Whatever their experience of love at the moment, what these people showed me—in their struggle and with their longing—was that we all have a tremendous need for love, love that fills our hearts, exhilarates our bodies, and nourishes our spirits.

As I worked with these people, however, what became apparent to me was how little we know about how to achieve the feelings and the experience, the solace, delight, and consolation that we would like our loves to grant us. We have been taught how to balance a checkbook, stamp out ring around the collar, and put together a gourmet meal, but we have never been taught how to create at truly loving relationship. Instead, with the help of romance novels, popular music, and the movies, we imagine that without any effort on our parts love will solve all our problems and make all our dreams come true.

Real love is more than a feeling, more than a magical interlude of emotional exhilaration that passes when the full moon fades to a sliver. Love is an array of behaviors, attitudes, and knowings, the practice of which creates and sustains the state of what we call love. Love, in the form of a relationship that satisfies, supports, and heals, is the product of intricate effort. In a very real sense, true love is a labor of love and it comes into being only when we realize that love, as well as being a gift, is also an undertaking.

For true love asks of us, as well as delivers to us. It asks that we alter our perspective about ourselves, the people we love, the world, and the human condition; that we learn things we are perhaps reluctant to know, or didn't imagine we needed to know. It requires us to change our behaviors, public and private, emotional and spiritual. It invites us to stretch as well as to reach, to nurture as well as to receive. It asks us to be kind, to be real, to be imaginative, thoughtful, attentive, intuitive, disciplined, daring. It instructs us in the art of being human.

This little book is also an invitation for you to change your beliefs about love itself—to see it not as a panacea for self-gratification, but as a power with an infinite capacity to utterly alter our lives. It is because we sense love's power to transform that we are constantly seeking to be in its midst, to partake of the blessings it can confer.

We are not here simply to be given love; we must also become loving. True love is conscious love, and conscious loving—the knowing and doing of a wide range of seemingly impossible tasks on behalf of one another—is the spiritual art form of the twentieth century.

The love in whose presence we stand must also inhabit us. For it is in loving, as well as in being loved, that we become most truly ourselves. No matter what we do, say, accomplish, or become, it is our capacity to love that ultimately defines us. In the end, nothing we do or say in this lifetime will matter as much as the way we have loved one another.

THE
CONDITIONS
OF LOVE

Love Is a Process, Not a Destination

We often think, at least unconsciously, that when we finally fall in love and decide to share our lives with another person, everything in our lives will fall into place. We'll "settle down," as we say, and, the implication is, we'll stay settled until "death do us part."

I call this the Shoe Box Notion of love. In this view, a relationship is like a shoe box or some other rather small container in which you keep something precious like your wedding bouquet. You wrap the flowers in tissue paper, put them in a box, put on the lid, place the box on a shelf, and hope the contents will stay just as they are forever and a day.

Unfortunately, this is precisely how many of us think about relationships. We put our love in a shoe box, stash it, and imagine we can retrieve it unchanged anytime we want. We think we don't have to do anything to make sure it doesn't get moldy or moth-eaten.

In truth, however, a relationship is a process and not a destination. It begins with a love that captures our attention and ignites our passion, and goes through the innumerable and unending undulations and permutations that give it texture, character, and spice, and which, without our necessarily liking or expecting it, shape and reshape the two people who created it.

Consciously or unconsciously we undertake many things in

our relationships. We review our history with our parents, we heal old wounds from childhood. In loving, we deliver ourselves to the nurturance and example of our beloved which enables us to develop numerous suppressed or abandoned aspects of ourselves. All these miracles of personal transformation occur precisely because, and only when, we abandon the notion that a particular relationship is a concrete monument occupying a fixed point in the universe.

A relationship is about movement, growth; it is a holy interpersonal environment for the evolution of two souls. The changes it goes through as an entity in itself are the measure of the changes being undertaken by the individuals in it. What we ask of our relationships is the measure of what they ask of us, and of what, in time, we will each become.

Therefore, remember that love is a process, and celebrate the changes it invites. To do so is always to be open to becoming much more than you were. To resist is to diminish yourself, to become, in the end, much less than you could be.

Everybody Needs More Love

In our relationships, that special, protective place we hope will be the fulfillment of all our hopes and dreams, we're all looking for the love we never got (or never got enough of) when we were children. Unfortunately, in the midst of striving for what we need and want, it's easy to forget that the other person over there could use some more love too.

In relationships, as everywhere else in life, we each tend to think that we're the only one who's got it (the problem, the cold), or had it (the bad day at work) or needs it (more love). But that's just not the way it is.

Everybody needs more love. More love. More love. More love. The truth is that nobody had a perfect childhood and none of us got enough praise, attention, recognition, affection, coddling, cuddling, blessing, or encouragement. We *all* need more now.

Keeping in mind that everybody is as needy as you are is a way of making sure that the love you give is equal to the love you take. This goes a long way toward keeping us from being Scrooges in love, so afraid we won't get ours that we become withholding and stingy, thereby reducing both partners to desperate love-starved babies.

It also insures that we are careful to do all those things that are the outward expression of feelings of love we have inside. We often make the mistake of assuming that, just because we love someone, he or she knows it and feels it—no special behavior is needed. But the experience of feeling loved is developed through a myriad of specific attitudes, acts, and ministrations that are the playing out of what we hold in our heart. We need not only to "love" one another, but to act that love out in consistent ways.

So, remember that the other person needs just as much love as you do, and be generous with your love in every way—with praise, kisses, compliments, music, lights, camera, action. Love with silence, kindness, color, meditation, prayer. Love in ways you haven't even dreamed of yet.

The more love you give, the more you will receive; the more love is given and received, the more it will abound; the more love abounds, the sweeter life will be; the sweeter life is, the more love itself will be the atmosphere we live and breathe.

Everybody's Wounded: The Torn Ear Theory of Love

When we fall in love, we unconsciously or consciously expect that the other person will be perfect—the perfect companion, playmate, friend, lover, parent for our children. It's when we hit up against the truth that the person we love is a mortal human being and not the projection of our wildest unbridled fantasies that relationships run into problems. Suddenly the knight on the white horse has cracks in his armor and Rapunzel in her tower has burrs in her beautiful long hair.

This is the time to pull out the Torn Ear Theory of Love; it's a great antidote to outrageous expectations. The Torn Ear Theory asks you to accept that the person you love isn't perfect and to love him or her anyway. It was named in honor of my old cat, Max. In his youth, Max was a beautiful boy, a Maine coon cat with eyes to die for. He had style, he had class; he had winning social ways, a certain refinement of features, an admirable purr, and a mighty hunting wisdom. I, of course, loved him.

But one day in his adolescence, Max got into a street fight. He came home with his ear all bloody, torn half way down to his head. The wound eventually healed, but the tear was always there. The question, of course, was did I, would I, could I, still love Max now that the he was obviously flawed? And the answer was, and still is, of course, yes.

The truth is that all of us are like Max—we're all wounded, we all have torn ears in one form or another, scars on our spirits (and sometimes our bodies) where the ravages of childhood have left their mark: a tattered sense of self-esteem, embarrassment about a particular physical imperfection, fear that we may be unlovable, shame about some limited achievement, the feeling that, try as we might, we won't get anywhere in life. It's these things that cause us to act in less than perfect ways.

What is sad but true, however, is that we imagine or assume that the other person doesn't have any wounds. We forget that the desperate, afraid, and sad little child in ourselves has a counterpart in the person we love, a child who can match us scar for scar and flaw for flaw.

Remembering that nobody's perfect is the talisman that will help you accept your beloved in his or her imperfections. It will breed patience to remember that you are not the only person who is suffering. At a more profound level, it will encourage you to take the time to get acquainted with one another's wounds, to discover how you can nurture, cherish, and respond.

Best of all, remembering we all have torn ears will leave you feeling less alone. For to know that the person you love is also wounded is to know that we suffer not in isolation, but in unison.

Everybody Has Circumstances

In love we often expect our partners to do, stop doing, be, say, give, or receive whatever we want them to without remembering that they have lives of their own. Unfortunately (and fortunately) a relationship isn't a free-for-all for the indulgence by the other person of every one of our needs and whims, whether emotional or practical. Everybody has circumstances, pragmatic realities he or she is caught up in, shaped by, and trying more or less successfully to manage. This means that the person we love will not always be available or able to love us precisely at the time or in the ways we want.

Circumstances can seem so overwhelming—being stuck for years in a dead-end job to put the kids through college; having to cope with an aging mother who has Alzheimer's disease; trying to get a degree while working full-time—that we forget our partner has circumstances too. Because life can be so difficult, we want to be delivered and, in the love-should-give-us-everything mode, we expect to be saved by the person we love. If he really loved me he'd get us out of debt forever; if she really loved me she'd have sex with me whenever I want it.

Holding these hopes is a way of not acknowledging one of the basic disappointing facts of life: Life isn't fair. The burdens on all of us are enormous. Chances are that our loved ones, just like ourselves, are trying to cope with everything in the best way they know how.

Just like each of us, our partners have to suffer the wretched little insults of daily life: the conked-out battery, the office full of cigarette smoke, the put-down from the boss, the gravy stain on the new white shirt. She's had a bad day at work; his father is dying from cancer; and nobody's got enough energy to come home and make dinner.

Unfortunately, it's all too easy to forget about the other person's circumstances when we're at the effect of our own. I have a friend who used to have endless fights with her husband about his never being home until after 8 p.m. Finally he said to her, "Do you think I WANT to work so late every night? I'm sick to death of my job. But between sending you to graduate school and supporting the kids, I can't afford to quit." When she realized that he was as much a victim of circumstance as she was, she stopped picking on him and started giving him empathy and encouragement. Interestingly enough, not long after, he found a number of ways to come home earlier.

Remembering that everybody has circumstances is a way of joining each other in the human condition. When we acknowledge in our hearts, and through our actions, that the other person is also at the effect of daily life, we create another form of bonding. Instead of being at odds, we realize we're all in this together. We recognize that we neither live, love, labor, nor suffer alone.

Your Sweetheart Isn't You

It may seem absurdly obvious that your sweetheart isn't you, but one of the worst mistakes you can make in love is to generalize on the basis of yourself; that is, to presume that your partner is exactly like you in terms of hurts, habits, preferences, hopes, and expectations. Indeed, we fall in love with, and are mesmerized by, the magic of another human being precisely because that person is different from us. But all too often once we're ensconced in an intimate relationship, we tend to behave as if our mate is, or should be, an extension of ourselves.

This is visible in the matrimonial "we." "We don't like big cities." "We don't like swordfish." "We always . . ." "We never . . ." And it's invisible, but nonetheless present, in our private assumptions: "Because I like vacations in the mountains, so should you"; "Because I get up at the crack of dawn, so should you"; "Because I want kids, you should too"; "Because I love my mother, you will too"; "Because I express love in words, you will too." Countless fights come out of these seemingly harmless presumptions that because I do, so will (or should) you.

The consequence of these assumptions is that most people are giving and doing what they would like to receive in the form they would like to receive it in, rather than doing what the person they're related to wants. As a result, a lot of fights are occurring because partners aren't getting their needs met. They escalate because the person not getting his needs met complains, and the other person gets angry because what she perceives as a precious gift has just been rejected.

This kind of expecting the other person to be a clone of ourselves is an emotional hangover from infancy when, indeed, we were the center of the universe. When we were babies, the world DID revolve around us—if we woke up screaming at 5 a.m., then everybody else woke up too. But in adulthood, whenever you treat your sweetheart as if he or she is you, you disenfranchise him or her from the right to be a separate self. You reduce the person by your side to a kind of non-entity. You say, in effect, it's only my consciousness and preferences that matter here—what you feel or think is irrelevant.

The antidote to this stultifying situation is to learn to do one very simple thing: inquire. Explore. Ask. Let curiosity be your guide to finding out what your mate wants and needs from you. The more you know precisely who he or she is, the less you'll make this person-erasing mistake.

In the long run, remembering that the person you love is not you is a way of exposing yourself to the joy of knowing another soul in the truth and beauty of his or her own uniqueness. And it's celebrating the difference that's really what love's all about.

Your Sweetheart Isn't Psychic

If I had a dollar for every time somebody said to me: "But why do I have to ask? He should know what I feel/want/think," I could give King Midas a run for his money and live in a castle built of gold bricks.

Love does a great many magical things, but it doesn't turn us into psychic wizards. We need to *tell* each other what we want and *ask* for what we need. And I mean TELL and ASK. If nothing but the blue angora sweater will do for your 30th birthday—SAY that or you may end up with a set of kitchen canisters. If you want your darling to wear the black silk strapless dress to the office Christmas party, TELL her or she might just show up in that flowery number you hate. Not because he or she doesn't love you, but because he or she isn't psychic.

People often think that getting what you ask for makes the gift less special, but, in fact, discovering that the person you love has loved you enough to hear what you want, and gone to the trouble of giving it to you, is often even more special. It means that he or she wants to please you enough to give you your true heart's desire, whether that's a new living room couch, some time alone, that wild pair of earrings, or just a shoulder to cry on.

Of course wanting your sweetheart to be psychic is a wonderful fantasy. It would be great if he or she knew everything you wanted and could make it magically appear. Letting go of the dream that your honey will "just know" is really letting go of the childhood fantasy that your parents would always know exactly what you wanted. It's sad to think that love has limits, that getting what we want takes effort, but it does.

And once you've mourned your fantasy, remembering your sweetheart isn't psychic will encourage you to be more forthright and adventurous in expressing your needs and desires, which will make it more likely that the other person will meet them. Receiving what you want will make your heart soft and happy and open. You'll feel more loving and more love will start flowing back to you. So what's stopping you from asking? To remind yourself, put a note on your refrigerator that says: MY SWEETHEART ISN'T PSYCHIC!

ASSUMPTIONS ARE DANGEROUS
TO YOUR LOVE LIFE

Assumptions—saying something that presumes you know what another person is thinking, feeling, or doing—always hurt the person about whom they're made and create a barrier to intimacy. Remarks such as: "You don't care about me as much as I do about you"; "You don't have to worry about money"; "Work's a lot easier for you"; "You never listen"; "You don't have much to do today" all have the effect of closing down the other person and limiting reality to our interpretation of it. Basically we are saying, "I know who you are and what's going on with you and I don't need your version of the story."

Assumptions can feel like a violation of spirit to the person who is theoretically being perceived. They are a reduction of the true complexity of reality and a negation of the other person's essence. Many of us experienced these kinds of dismissing assumptions from our parents—"You're lazy; you'll never amount to anything"—and so we can be very easily hurt when someone assumes things about us that aren't true.

I was at a friend's house recently and witnessed the following conversation:

Martha: "I know you came home late from work just to torture me You're still angry about last night and you just wanted to punish me some more."

Fred: "Well, actually..."

Martha: "Come on, I know you're still mad. Stop pretending."

Fred: "I am not angry. Actually, there was head-on collision on the freeway right in front of me. Two people were killed. I had to drive into town to call the police."

Fred had been really shaken up by the accident, but rather than asking why he was late and then attempting to comfort him, Martha came on with a load of negative assumptions. That in turn made Fred angry and the situation deteriorated from there.

Assumptions take away our uniqueness and freedom of expression. They close off possibilities by making people withdraw and hide out even more. Eliminating assumptions opens the flow of real conversation in which lovers can show their real selves, and discover the beautiful particulars of one another.

COMMUNICATION IS THE
INTERPERSONAL MIRACLE

Far and away, the thing people complain most about in their relationships is "lack of communication." What they are really saying is that they don't feel truly known in ways that make them feel close, loved, christened. This is because most people don't believe they can be known. In our secret heart of hearts we all fear that we are alone in the universe and that no one will really understand us. While of course it is true that no one can ever know us exactly, down to the marrow of our bones, we can be known to a surprisingly wonderful degree if we are willing to take the risk of revealing who we are.

Contrary to our myths and expectations, communication isn't just talking, getting your own point across or being sure you've been heard. Far more then we imagine, communication is also receptive. It is listening, taking in, absorbing, and allowing yourself to be changed by what has been said to you. Without listening, talking can be a one sided enterprise, leaving the arch of communication incomplete. But when talking *and* listening occur, a conversation gains antiphony and both partners have the sense that they now occupy a common ground.

True communication, the kind we are all seeking, is a bonding of spirits. Through what we tell one another, we come to know how the person we love thinks, feels, and is likely to behave in any given circumstance. True communication is connecting at the level where the solitariness of individual boundaries is blurred and we know from the inside that we are in touch with the essence of the other.

This place of deep connection and interpersonal fulfillment doesn't just happen. It is arrived at through the steady practice of the art of communication on the intellectual, sexual, and emotional planes.

Communication takes courage. It requires a reaching beyond the trivial for the deeper truth of who you are and what you feel, and the willingness to take the risk of showing yourself to the other person. True communication is also receptive. It indicates that you love enough to be affected—moved, changed, enlarged, transformed—by what you have heard.

Because in its quintessence communication has the capacity to bond us at the deepest, most unspoken levels, true communication is an interpersonal miracle. It allows us to get inside one another's skins, and to know and be known truly by another human being. It is the means by which we throw open the windows of our own souls to let the light of another soul shine in.

Communication Is a Revelation, Not a Contest

We're all desperate to be heard, sensed, and responded to, but far too often we are frustrated in this attempt. That's because most of us don't really know how to communicate. The talking most of us do, the filling up of interpersonal air time, doesn't necessarily mean that anything meaningful has been said, or that anybody has been heard.

True communication is a revelation, not a contest. Rather than a meaningless, mindless, or egotistical barrage of verbiage, it is an exchange of feelings, and information that can open both people to more awareness and love. True communication has four parts:

1. The message: Words that are spoken to convey a specific meaning. Usually messages fall into one of five categories: a feeling, e.g., "I'm disappointed because I didn't get the raise"; a piece of information: "The show starts at one"; a request: "Can we plan a vacation for after your busy season at work?"; a plea: "Please tell me I'll pass the CPA exam"; or a preference: "I like the plain wallpaper better."

2. Listening: The receptive state of endeavoring to apprehend the meaning of what is being said. In listening you

try to take in what the other person is saying, rather than just responding with a facile retort;

3. Responding: Communicating in words what you think you have heard and revealing how it has made you feel;

4. Acknowledgement: Stating that you have received the response and indicating the way it has affected you.

Only when all four elements—speaking, listening, responding, and acknowledging—are present has a communication been completed. In speaking we tell who we are and what we feel. In listening we receive the meaning of what has been said and a sense of who the other person is. In responding we show that we have received the message and that we care. In acknowledging the response we show that we appreciate the other's caring.

True communication seeks to see more and show more, rather than to defend the status quo. It looks for the revelation, the new thing to be learned, and then answers with a fresh response so even more can be revealed. It is galvanized by compassion, the state of heart that allows you to seek the truth, whether you are speaking or listening, and deepens the level of intimacy by expanding the range of what can be revealed.

RELATIONSHIPS HAVE SEASONS

Love is not just the ebullient rush of new passion, it is also the gathering of deep knowing, a knowledge that develops through the testing of sorrows and the challenge of duress. Relationships start with the spring green energy of new love and lustful ardor, and move, in time, through a variety of seasons. As love progresses, there's more (or less) time to spend together, periods when if feels as if you have nothing to say to one another, times when you think there's no way you could possibly live without him or her.

People and circumstances from the outside yank at our loves: jobs, in-laws, children, financial worries, health problems, the losses of separation and death. Change can wreak havoc with the stability of a relationship, as a new career, a remodeling project, or a move to a different town can bring on a crisis of discomfort we can all too easily blame on our partners. Even our own fears and inabilities can make us doubt our loves and, from time to time, unconsciously try to dismantle them.

Many couples go through difficult patches, times when they begin to wonder if they will ever regain the tender, excited, and passionate feelings that brought them together. Sometimes these crisis points seem almost unbearable, but in fact they indicate that the relationship is going through an emotional convulsion. It is shedding an old skin, a familiar way of being together that needs to be revised so that the partners and the relationship itself can be elevated to a much higher level of functioning.

When we go through one of these spells of feeling fractured or disillusioned, we need to remember that just as in nature there is a changing of the seasons, so the spring of new love will mature to the summer of depth and passion, and the autumn of open hearth and quiet companionship may also give way to a winter that can leave you feeling cold and estranged.

If you remember that relationships have seasons, you won't expect your relationship to stand unchanged. Instead you will welcome the changes and look for the resources in yourself that will make you equal to them.

So be brave about your love. Look at the difficult times as invitations to transformation. Hold fast in hard times, remembering that the things that first drew you together are still there to be drawn upon. And know that, like the seasons, the beautiful times, enhanced by the history and the suffering you have shared, will surely return to bless and ignite your love again.

THE
PRACTICES
OF LOVE

Nourishing Your Loving Self

LOVE YOURSELF

All too many of us consider love to be the miracle by which, finally, we will become complete human beings. This is the fixer-upper notion of love, the idea that we're not all right as we are, but if we can just get loved by somebody, then that will prove we're ok.

Ironically, however, in order to be well loved, you need first to love yourself. For in love, we get not necessarily what we deserve, but what we THINK we deserve. Just as Harry Homeowner who has a house that's worth one million dollars might sell it for only $500,000 if that's all he thinks it's worth, so the person who under-estimates his or her own value will always be shortchanged in love.

Love begets love. If you don't think well of yourself, you can't be positively affected by the person who is celebrating you for the specialness you don't believe you have. If you don't know, and love, what's important, special, precious, and beautiful about yourself, you can be sure you will not be serenaded, sent roses, lauded, paraded, or daily smothered in kisses by someone who does.

Loving yourself is knowing yourself, enjoying and valuing your-self, and understanding that self-knowledge is a lifelong personal enterprise. It means that you appreciate yourself at least as much as you value your honey, that you know he or she is as lucky in love as you believe you are. It means you measure your strengths and weaknesses neither with the abuse of self-deprecation nor the insanity of ego mania, but with genuineness, with accuracy. Loving yourself is recognizing your gifts and talents, and putting them to good use, acknowledging your flaws, and forgiving yourself for them. Loving yourself is reaching for more, for the best, in yourself.

So often we put up with shabby treatment in love because we don't believe we deserve better. But self-love is always the model for the love you may reasonably expect, the true measure of the love you will give and get. Your heart can only hold as much love as you believe it can. So treat yourself better, believe you deserve to be treated well, and you will get treated ever more wonderfully in love.

Say What You Feel

Feelings reside in us like a river and pass through our consciousness in an ever-moving flow. They run the range from fear, sadness, shame, and anger to joy, delight, exuberance, and playfulness. At any moment we can reach in and discover what we are feeling. Saying what you feel is giving audible language to the flow of feelings, discovering and articulating those emotions that are the constant undercurrent of our lives.

Revealing these emotional tides to the person you love is a way for you to continue to endear yourself to and amaze your partner. We often think that intimacy is created merely by falling in love or by what we do, plan, buy, or pursue together. But it is actually the getting to know another person through the intricate texture of his or her emotions that makes us feel truly connected. In fact an intimate relationship at its core is a process of trading feelings to a high degree.

Indeed it is the revelation of feelings that deepens intimacy with one another. For it is in our feelings, our capacity to be delighted and disappointed, to grieve, to be afraid, to want, to feel the loss of, that we dip into the common human stream and connect with one another at the deepest level. This is why, when you say what you feel, your partner discovers him or herself through you.

Paradoxically and sadly it's often when we love someone that we tend to not share our emotions and to revert to information-laden conversation because it just doesn't occur to us that the other person's interested in what we're sad, happy, scared, or angry about. In this way, proximity can breed not knowing.

But believe it or not, it is precisely this experience that your beloved wants. She or he *wants* to see the kaleidoscope of your inner emotional contents. It's what makes you loveable.

If it's difficult for you to express your emotions, what you need to know is that it will be worth it to step into the curiously unfamiliar waters and discover the treasures at your depths. Not only will your partner be pleased to connect with you in this way, but the experience of discovering and identifying your feelings will give you a greater sense of richness about your own inner life. Therefore, let the person you love enter the underground stream of your feelings so he can cherish you, so she can love you even more, by starting to say, exactly and always, whatever is in your heart and mind.

Ask for What You Need

Asking for what you need is just that: stating that there is something amiss about which you need some care or response. "Would you please close the window? I'm freezing." "I need you to hold me; I'm scared." "Will you give me a back rub? My shoulder hurts." "Can you skip the ball game and go to the movies with me? I've been home alone all day and I'm stir crazy."

Asking for what you need is such a simple yet difficult thing that most of us rarely, if ever, do it. In fact, it is so hard (or easy) that most of us would rather try almost anything else than to ask quite simply and directly for precisely what we need. We would rather presume that our sweetheart will know without our telling, or hope that in time our spouse will, by osmosis, figure it out. Often we'd just as soon give up on getting the thing we need than to actually have to ask for it.

We don't like to ask because we think of asking as revealing neediness—which is precisely what it is. Asking means we are in a vulnerable state and that we are hoping the other person will care enough to minister to us in our pitiful, imperfect, and inadequate condition.

Unfortunately, when we're in love we can get into the strange frame of mind that somehow we ought to be perfect and invulnerable. It's as if we believe that one of the requirements of love is that only people who need absolutely nothing can be loved. In reality, love ministers to our vulnerabilities and the gift of love is that it can do for us what we are unable to do for ourselves.

Asking for what you need reveals the true fragileness of your humanity, and invites the person who loves you to expand the range of his or her own. Responding to a stated request not only gives the needy person the relief of having the need fulfilled, but it also gives the giver a sense of being able to be effective, to offer a gift of value. On these occasions, you are both enjoined to expand the range of your love and your humanity.

However, just because you ask for something doesn't necessarily mean that you will get it. Asking in itself doesn't guarantee results—you may ask your spouse to buy you a Porsche, but that doesn't mean he or her has the wherewithal to provide it. When you're just learning to ask, not getting results can be discouraging. Just remember that asking does greatly improve your chances; the more you ask, the more the odds increase that you will get your needs met.

BE EMOTIONALLY BRAVE

Too many of us are emotional chickens, afraid to communicate what we are really feeling. Emotional chickens are afraid that what they disclose will be ignored, made fun of, or ridiculed, so rather than taking the risk of spitting it out—whatever it is—they just keep quiet. Often they even defend their shut-down stance, saying that talking about feelings never does any good anyway. Yet emotions kept in, stuffed down, or anaesthetized in various ways always take a physiological, emotional, and spiritual toll on us.

Being an emotional chicken has old, sad origins. It begins when we aren't listened to as children, when we were told that the things we said were unimportant or when we sensed that no one could feel with us in our private anguish. Feeling this way made us scared. And fear taught us to keep our thoughts and feelings to ourselves.

Being emotionally brave means that now, in spite of the possible adverse effects, you will risk saying the thing that may leave you feeling exposed, and trust in a happy outcome. Chances are things will turn out well, for revealing vulnerabilities most often brings couples closer together.

For example, Lana was afraid to tell Ron that she had been sexually abused as a child. She was terrified he would think of her as soiled, that he would be disgusted and reject her. Instead, when she finally worked up the nerve to tell him, he was filled with compassion. He held her very tenderly and told her how sorry he was, and she had a healing cry in his arms.

It isn't only the big secrets that we're afraid to tell. Many of us are uncomfortable saying anything that might be construed as even slightly confrontational: "I don't want to go to the Taj Mahal Cafe. I want to go to the Bean Sprout Club for dinner"; "I'm angry at you for not making love to me last night"; "Thursday's my birthday and I hope you'll remember because I'll be terribly disappointed if you don't." But of course it's precisely the things you are afraid of telling your sweetheart that will show him or her who you really are.

Here's how to be emotionally brave: Whenever you're having the slightly unsettled feeling that comes from not saying what's on your mind, try asking yourself: *What is it that I'm not saying?* Usually the words are right in your mind like in one of those little cartoon balloons. Then ask yourself: *Why am I not saying it right NOW?* Maybe there's a good reason—he just got fired from his job, the kids are both crying, you have to walk out the door in five minutes for a business meeting, your mother-in-law is on the phone. In such cases, you probably should hold your comments for later. But if there isn't a good, practical reason for not speaking NOW, just open your mouth and spit out the words that are dying to get out. You'll feel better—and your relationship will also get better as it holds more of the truth of who you and your sweetheart really are.

REVEAL WHAT MAKES YOU FEEL LOVED

Kirsten fell in love with Tommy because on the first date he showed up at her house wearing a red and black checked flannel shirt, carrying two bottles of German beer, a box of crackers and a wedge of limburger cheese. "It was great," she said, "he believed me when I told him I loved limburger cheese."

Her best friend Phyllis wasn't impressed. "If somebody showed up to court me with limburger cheese," she said, "I might not be insulted but I certainly wouldn't be happy. Give me a bouquet of pink carnations any day."

As the difference between Kristen and Phyllis demonstrate, love doesn't have its effect if it doesn't come in the form we need, no matter how much the person who loves us is trying. And all too many of us are sitting around waiting for, or worse yet expecting, that our darlings will automatically know precisely what makes us feel loved, and exactly when, where, how, and in what form to deliver it to us.

The message here is what I call The Limburger Cheese Theory of Love. It states that if limburger cheese is what makes you feel loved, then you'd better tell your mate to give you limburger cheese. It means quite simply that everybody has his or her own particular ordinary (or extraordinary) preferences, and that nobody's going to make you feel loved if you don't tell him or her exactly what your preferences are.

Whether we know it or not we all have a secret laundry list of what makes us feel loved: his carrying your photo in his wallet; her scratching the back of your head; his cooking dinner for you; her wearing your favorite blue tee shirt to the gym. What's on your list? Think about it, write it down, and share it with your partner.

Of course you'll never be loved exactly, entirely, always, or precisely in the ways you want. But give your sweetheart a chance to make you feel as loved as possible by telling or showing him or her exactly the items on your list.

Although people often say to me, "If I have to tell him or her, then it doesn't count," the truth is that nobody can guess the myriad little do-dahs on your particular list. Love laundry lists are as different as our noses, and if you wait for the other person to figure what makes you feel loved, you could live your whole life without getting what you want. Getting the things on your list really *does* make you feel loved, even if you have to nail the list up on the bathroom wall or publish it in the Sunday *Times.*

So give your sweetheart a chance to really love you. Make your love laundry list.

EXPOSE YOUR SECRET LOVE SCENARIO

We each have a private love scenario, a fantasy about what would make us feel really loved. It represents the fulfillment of our heart's desire, the things we believe could never occur but in our heart of hearts hope will happen anyway. Whatever its magical components, it's often so secret that we haven't even consciously identified it for ourselves.

Exposing your secret scenario is letting yourself and your sweetheart know exactly the thing, or things, that would make you feel loved and special, whether that's an object (the monogrammed golf clubs), an attitude (an endless array of adoring words), an atmosphere (the exact kind of music), or a sensual preference (the precise way you would like to make love).

It may include the dream of a particular occasion, or may refer to a lifestyle, a special set of circumstances, or an emotional way of being: "What would make me feel really loved is if the woman in my life would sleep all night with her head on my chest. Every night"; "I want a lawn party for my birthday—white dresses, lanterns in the trees, a dance band playing Count Basie songs in the background"; "I've always wanted a woman who would sit in the stands while I play polo"; "I've always wanted to go to Paris with someone I love."

Whatever your personal particulars are, your spouse needs to know them. Our fantasies can't always be fulfilled, but the chances of having them come true immediately drop to zero if we don't speak up about what they are.

Allowing yourself to discover your scenario and taking the risk of revealing it to your spouse in all it's delicious extravagance is the first step in making it come true. For when your sweetheart begins to know your heart's desire, he or she can begin to make it come true. Perhaps she can't sleep all night with her head on your chest, but she can do it for at least a few minutes every night. Perhaps he can't afford all those roses right now, but he can give you the first dozen now and remember to bring you the rest when he's flush.

So don't keep your secret love scenario a secret. Tell all. Give your partner a chance to love you in exactly the ways you would like. Risk feeling absolutely, meltingly happy!

Go Easy on Yourself

All of us know what a morbidly delicious temptation it can be to beat yourself up about almost anything that goes wrong in your relationship, or for that matter, in life in general.

If you have a fight, or if you're too chicken to pick a fight, if you have an orgasm or if you don't, if it takes you forever to decide something or you decide impulsively, if you waste money or are a miser, if you're a neatness fanatic or a slob—whatever your habits, predilections, attitudes or expectations, you may find yourself blaming yourself for whatever goes awry in your relationship.

Rob blamed himself for years, because whenever he and Jane had to make a decision about anything really important, he mulled it over for weeks. He analyzed it, slept on it, consulted with his, as he called them, "secret agents," then, long after Jane had made up her mind and was, as it were, tap-tapping her pencil on the kitchen table in impatience, he'd finally make his decision.

Once "his stewing" as Jane referred to it meant that they lost their chance to buy what they both had thought was their dream house. Rob was so busy analyzing the comparables, checking out loans, that three weeks into his process the house was snapped up by somebody else. Although Jane was disappointed, she actually recovered fairly quickly. "These things happen," she said, "don't worry, we'll find another perfect house."

But long after they'd moved into a wonderful house, Rob was still beating himself up about the house his indecisiveness had lost. "I should have listened to Jane. I shouldn't be so perfectionistic about every single decision. I'm just a fuddy duddy, why can't I just make up my mind?"

The reality is that no matter what our style, no matter what we do precipitously, or fail to do in time or in the right way, we're all doing the best we can. Beating yourself up, blaming yourself, focusing endlessly on your faults—the way you might have been or should have been, done it or not done it—never improves the situation.

Look at yourself with compassion. Enjoy your curious little idiosyncrasies. Acknowledge that it's just fine to be you. Let it be all right that you're different from everybody else. As the Yiddish adage asks, "If I be like him, then who will be like me?"

Being easy on yourself means that you accept yourself as you are, that you forgive yourself for your mistakes and go on, lovingly acknowledging your foibles, your idiosyncratic style. Only by being gentle with yourself can you also be good natured and forgiving with the person you love. So give yourself a break and decide that you're just fine exactly as you are.

Cherishing Your Beloved

CELEBRATE THE EXCEPTIONAL

We all fall in love for a reason. There is something so unique and rare in the person you love that no matter what his flaws or her shortcomings, you return again and again in your mind to that ineffable quality which, for you anyway, is the essence of why you fell in love in the first place.

Taking note of that quality, remarking on it to your beloved, talking about it to your friends and children, will help keep your love fresh and vivid. We all enjoy hearing how wonderful we are: "You're so organized. I'd never even make it to the office with my briefcase if it weren't for you"; "You are so calm. Without your level head I'd probably be in the loony bin by now"; "You always know just the right thing to say to make me feel better."

Compliments are the verbal nourishment of the soul. They generate self-esteem, and in a very subtle way create a person in the full spectrum of his or her essence. Compliments invite the person who is complimented to embrace a new perception of him or herself. And just as layers and layers of nacre form a pearl over an irritating grain of sand, so compliments collect around us, developing us in all our beauty.

Celebrating the exceptional will make you aware not only of the value of the other person but also of your own specialness. To contemplate the uniqueness of your mate is, at the same time, to inform yourself about your own fine qualities. For the exceptionalness of your beloved is a reflection of yourself; you would not be in the arms of this incredible person if there weren't something very special about you. To honor your wife's beauty is to be reminded of your own worthiness. To relish your husband's sensitivity is to be made aware that you are the kind of person in whose presence such emotional elegance can flourish.

In such ways do we confirm that we are not only lucky in love, but worthy of being loved. To see the appropriateness of your being together is to have a sense of hope and joy about your mutual love. Therefore, lavish praise on the person you love, and the blessings will come back to you a thousand fold.

Praise the Ordinary

Life as we know it unfortunately includes a multitude of things which are boring, tedious, and at times downright offensive. Cleaning up after the dog mess, playing Chutes and Ladders for the 30th time that day with your three-year-old son, having to cook dinner at 8 p.m. after an exhausting day at the office—none of these things are what give life its special joy.

That as a part of loving one another we do, and continue to do, these ordinary and sometimes spirit-crunching things is a testament to the good-natured generosity of love, and to the lengths love is willing to go to show its human kindness.

Praising these ordinary acts— "You did a great job on the dinner for my boss," "Thanks, honey, for cleaning out the closet," "It means so much to me that you always have milk in the house for my coffee," "I appreciate your always paying the bills"—can make doing of the ordinary bearable. As my friend Kim the caterer says, "It's nice to be acknowledged for even the smallest of virtues."

When we get praised for such things not only are we given the sense that the prosaic things we do are appreciated, but also that our partner knows we do them out of love. In marriage especially, it is easy to dwindle into a maid or a handyman, to feel as if our only connection to each other is through the doing of domestic chores. But when we praise these ordinary undertakings, we acknowledge that they are not the highest callings we both can aspire to.

Praise makes the other person feel grateful for the opportunity to do the pedestrian and sometimes wretched little things of life. And because we articulate how much we value him or her for doing these simple things, we keep the pedestrian in its place and, by so doing, remember that we love one another for higher, deeper, and much more special reasons.

So don't take your loved one for granted—it's easy to forget in the press of daily life all the little things he or she does for you. Figure out a way to remember: tie a string around your finger, post a note on the mirror, write yourself a reminder and put it in your underwear drawer. Praising the ordinary is one truly simple way to keep up each other's spirits in the valleys of the mundane that lie between the peak experiences of special times.

DO THE EXTRAORDINARY
ORDINARY THING

Part of the graciousness of love is that it allows us to deepen the meaning of even the simplest gestures of ordinary life, to make the commonplace uncommon, to make the familiar magic. Doing the extraordinary ordinary thing is performing a commonplace service for no reason, and in these days of instant everything, the formerly ordinary has become extraordinarily special. It's a luxury to have a homemade pie, a hand-mended sock, a custom-made spice rack.

From time to time Jed gives Diane an envelope full of coupons, certificates in exchange for which he'll polish her shoes, sharpen the knives, plant the petunias in pots on the porch, and clean the ridiculously messy front hall closet. Joanne mends Steven's sweaters and sews his buttons on. Once a year when he's gone she'll spend a whole day going through his closet, repairing everything that needs attention. "It's the most special thing," Steven says, "so loving, because I know she doesn't really have the time."

Sometimes doing the extraordinary ordinary thing is simply creating an occasion to do some banal thing together. Whenever they have a dinner party, Belinda and Jim wash dishes together, even though they have a dishwasher. "We really enjoy it. There's something about the warm soapy water and the linen dish towels that makes everything seem easy. For us, it's a time to decompress, to talk about the people at the party, how we compare with our friends, to remind ourselves of what we have. Some really quite amazing things come out. Normally, we'd never take the time to say the things we say in these dishwashing gabs, but there's something so safe about just standing there together at the sink, letting our hair down."

By doing the extraordinary ordinary thing you communicate in a very simple way that you love one another. You remind yourselves that you have thrown your lot together, that you want to keep your life knitted up together for the long skein of the future. And since ordinary things refer in our unconscious to uncomplicated times, they're therefore a wonderful balm to over-stressed lives. They remind us that no matter how complicated life can get, some of the sweetest, most solacing gestures of love are really very simple.

BE A PERSON OF YOUR WORD

Words—and the way our actions do or don't stand behind their meaning—have an incredible capacity to wound us or to heal us. In a very real sense, words create reality. For we all invest one another's words with our hopes, fears, and expectations. Therefore, to keep love alive in your life, be a person of your word.

Being a person of your word creates faith in a relationship. It means that not only will you keep your promises, but in a more general sense, you will say what you intend and do what you say.

Nothing can erode a relationship as consistently or as deeply as too many words that mean nothing. For many of us, the biggest betrayals in our lives were delivered in the form of words that weren't true: "He said he was working late at the office, but all that time he was having an affair"; "My father promised to take me to Europe, but then he married my stepmother and went with her instead"; "She swore he was just a friend, but come to find out, she'd been in love with him for years."

Since we've all been wounded by words, when we encounter unkept promises, we can very quickly be shaken to the core. We'd all like to believe that we can expect endless emotional resilience from our partners, that it's acceptable time and time again to not quite say what we mean or say something that turns out not to be true.

But in reality, our hearts can only stand so many little white lies or unintentionally broken promises. At some point, our faith begins to be eroded and we begin to take note of the number of times our mate didn't do what he or she said, and in a very subtle way we begin to discount his or her words. Without even noticing it, we begin to not listen, to not trust even the things our partner may still really mean.

So, aside from the exceptions that are unavoidable—you promised to go to his college reunion and your back gave out the night before—make every effort to mean and do what you say. Being a person of your word will build a fortress of trust in your relationship, and that trust will allow you to truly savor the words of love and praise that are the treasured hallmark of an abiding love.

CRITICIZE ONLY IN PRIVATE

We all do things that are less than perfect—some of us talk too fast or interrupt constantly; others are perpetually late, sloppy about housekeeping or perfectionistic in our work habits. The things we do wrong are enough of an embarrassment to us that we certainly don't need to be reminded about them in public.

Registering such seemingly innocent or small time complaints as "You never remember to take out the garbage," or "You always spill on your new clothes; you're such a mess" even jokingly in the presence of friends, dinner guests, the plumber, your aunt, or a mother-in-law, is degrading to another person's essence. It has the effect of making him or her feel small, worthless, and punished in the presence of people among whom he or she would like to feel whole, effective, and worthy.

It doesn't do much to solidify your relationship either. How much would you feel like helping your wife take the car to the garage if, when you show up at her office, she says in front of her boss that she can't believe how long it took you to get here?

Reprimands always have painful reference to childhood. They harken back to a haunting sense of inadequacy, and the feelings of powerlessness that were the hallmarks of being small and at the mercy of our parents. For this reason, it is doubly painful to be reminded of our flaws, shortcomings, and failures in front of anyone except our intimate dear ones, whom we may legitimately hope will try to understand and forgive.

It is true that we all have creepy little inadequacies that bear remarking on, and when they are noted in private, we can be inspired to change. Indeed criticism, like encouragement, can shape the direction of our path and therefore serves a wonderfully creative function.

But when criticism is leveled in public, it diminishes our dignity and, far from correcting whatever needs to be improved, makes us skittish and afraid. We begin to feel that we're not acceptable as ourselves and eventually, in order to even up the situation, we may begin to withdraw our acceptance from our partner, until the public persona of our relationship is a catty downward spiral of teasing, judgments, and put downs.

Public maligning is the antithesis of loving support and closeness. Rather than being an invitation to change, reprimanding is a spirit-breaking act. Preserve your love by graciously keeping silent about the things you'd like to correct until you're in the privacy of one another's arms.

DO THE UNEXPECTED

Sarah surprised her husband, Matt, by appearing at his office on his birthday in black net stockings, top hat and tails, carrying a cake and singing "Happy Birthday."

Jim told Abby he had to pick up some film for his new camera and would she come along for the ride? Then he drove to the park, unloaded a picnic basket from the trunk of the car, revealed a gorgeous bouquet of red roses and, under the spreading elms, asked her to marry him.

Susie sometimes puts orange blossoms in Fred's bath water; Fred serenades Susie from their bedroom balcony. Shelly puts a love note into Bill's folded tee shirts; Bill buys Shelly new nightgowns "for absolutely no reason."

Everybody (well almost everybody) likes a surprise, the uninvited appearance of the totally unexpected, the unusual, the hidden treasure, the silver lining. The unanticipated event leaves us happily off kilter, so spice up your life by doing something completely different. Throw gardenia petals on the bed, put a love note in the freezer, read each other a bedtime story, bury tickets to the circus under the pillow, take your honey to a fortune teller, follow your sweetheart around for a whole day with a camera and make a photo essay of her life, leave a secret erotic message on his answering machine, call her at work just to tell her you love her, serve a candlelight dinner in bed. Pretend you're asleep and then wake your spouse up to make love.

Doing the unexpected has a number of beautiful effects. It gives you an opportunity to enjoy your own imagination and utilize your (perhaps neglected) creativity, it makes your partner feel special and it enlivens your love.

It's easy to get in a rut. But you can do the same old thing any old time. It's the exceptional that makes love feel like love and not just a two-person version of drab, dull, daily routine. So do the unexpected—whatever it is and as often as you can—and watch as love turns from dishwater dull to the sparkle of champagne.

BEHAVE YOURSELF IN PUBLIC

Your relationship, just like you, has a self-image. You and your beloved came together to express, among other things, the fact that the union of two people is a worthy and beautiful thing. Holding your relationship and the other person in high regard means you will also treat it in public as the treasure you know it to be.

Behaving yourself in public means you will not provocatively (or in any other way) flirt with somebody else, nor will you thoughtlessly compare your honey to others, make fun of the person you love, nor rudely fight in the presence of others.

Don't turn your darling into a sour puss at the party (or a disinterested lover when you get home) by staring too long at the statuesque blonde. Don't make your beloved feel inadequate by leaning too close or talking too long to the rock and roll star who just showed up at the benefit dinner. And don't make yourself look like you picked the wrong guy by putting your sweetheart down at the neighborhood Fourth of July barbecue.

Of course she has faults. Of course he isn't perfect. But nobody else needs to know it. Don't announce it to the world—it's none of their business. And don't compare your sweetheart's anything—looks, manners, attributes, foibles, or bank account—to anybody you met at the party. It hurts to be compared.

Most of all, don't stage your fights in public. The annual dinner of the Country Bar Association isn't Madison Square Garden. Just because you couldn't resolve your problems before you left home or your spouse said something at dinner to hurt you, doesn't mean you should try to have it out in front of an audience. Don't double the ignominy of your insults by letting other people cackle at them—keep your emotional dirty laundry at home.

When we behave badly in public, we make ourselves and our partner look like a fool—we're foolish for having chosen such an inadequate person, they're foolish for putting up with us maligning or mistreating them.

Flirting, comparing your partner with others, making fun of the person you love, and fighting in public are all practices that can put hairline cracks and scars in the emotional geology of your relationship. They're sleazy, unreasonable tests that nobody deserves to be put through.

Love needs to be nurtured, not threatened and abused. Behaving yourself in public means you care enough to keep your honey comfortable, care enough to have the outside world stand in honor—or in awe—of the person you chose and the relationship you created.

SHOWER EACH OTHER WITH KISSES

A relationship needs to be S.W.A.K. Remember that? It meant that the letter you sent, the words you wrote, and the feelings you had were made more dear because you sealed them with a kiss. Even when courtship is over, the love you live needs to be sealed and affirmed again and again with a multitude of kisses. For kisses, the loving embrace of the lips, are the sign, more than almost anything else, that we like, love, cherish, and adore the person we are kissing.

Kisses, like those little candy hearts on Valentine's Day, can carry all our little (and big and magnificent) messages of love. They are the sweetest, simplest, common denominator expression of love. Whenever we give them to one another we are nurturing our bond.

As kisses are the portal to erotic life in new romance, so they are the life support system of erotic passion in a long-time love. They are the emblem of passionate contact, the way we tell one another that we love and that we would like to make love.

But kisses aren't simply the key-card to erotic passion, and, once having entered the realm of sexual intimacy, we need to remember that kisses also have a power and a beauty of their own. Kisses can and should have a multitude of meanings. They can be the sign that true love is about to begin, they can be the connection of affection, they can be the counterpoint to passion. Wordless, they speak everything from "Honey, I'm home," to "Congratulations"; "I'm wild about you"; "Darling, I adore you"; "You're the one I desire"; "I'm yours"; to "I'm sorry." But whatever their specific function at the moment, kisses say we want to be attached to, come home to, and spiritually embrace the person we are kissing.

Kisses are the food of love. They make us feel . . . kissed. Chosen, desirable, powerful, beautiful, sensual, joyful, happy, carefree, invincible, LOVED. Kisses lift the level of our experience from daily and banal to delicious and extraordinary. Kisses capture our attention, and express our best intentions. So never underestimate the power of a kiss.

SPEAK THE LOVE WORDS

Everybody wants to hear how much, and precisely why, he or she is loved. Even when we've been chosen, even when we've tied the knot, we still need the verbal reassurance that we are loved. We need to be endeared, to feel that we are special, delightful, delicious, precious, irreplaceable to the one we love. We want to be singled out, to be told we are loved above all by the person who has chosen us.

We often think that having a feeling about someone is as good as saying it, but it isn't. Make no mistake—words mean a lot to us all. We all walk around with a huge collection of insecurities, and none of us is so sure, so cut and dried in our conviction about our own self-worth that we don't need the inspiration of being told every which way, over and over again, exactly why, how, and how much we are loved.

We need to be TOLD. And the words have to be heartfelt. There's just no comparison between the abstract "Of course I love you" and the direct "I love you. You're my darling. I want to be with you forever," no contest between silence and "You are the light of my life."

Even though some people may think it is corny, in the delicate layers of even the coolest of cucumber hearts is a lover who yearns to be adored. There's a hidden romantic in each of us, the person who fell in love, who was tantalized by music and moonlight, who waited breathlessly to hear the words that heralded new love: "I adore you. I can't live without you." And once wasn't—and never will be—enough. For even if we could, we don't want to have to keep faith about love. We want our hearts to be filled by hearing the love words over and over again.

So call your beloved by a special name and tell each other often what delights you about her, why you so deeply love him. Say the mushy/gushy things you thought people only said in movies—the more romantic, the more erotic, the more delicious, the better: "You are the woman of my dreams"; "I love you to pieces"; "You're my angel"; "You're such a wonderful man"; "You're a fabulous lover."

Love words are a tonic for love, an elixir for passion, a medicinal balm for fading romance. Life is infested with ordinariness and there isn't any reason why love should be also. Love is what we fall into in order to partake of magic; love is how we fly. And words are the wings of romance, the way in which, more than any other, we elevate ourselves above the grueling and pedestrian. Nothing can sustain the high pitch of romance better than beautiful love words, generously and endlessly spoken.

Say Please

It sounds incredibly simplistic, but our relationships would definitely improve if we remembered to say "Please." Please wake me up before you leave in the morning. Please close the door. Please call your mother and tell her we can't make it to the family dinner this week. Please help me cut back the vines. Please clean your own hairs out of the bathtub drain. Please make some appetizers for the office Christmas party. Please kiss me. Please come to bed.

While saying "Please" may seem unnecessary, something that you can just dispense with now that you know one another so well, or even a throwback to outdated childhood etiquette, it isn't. "Please" means you aren't taking the other person for granted. Rather, it says that consistently, in the tiniest of ways, you recognize that a relationship is, among other things, a constant interchange of kindnesses, things you do both easily or with great effort for each other.

"Please" is a safeguard password to insure you never allow your relationship to end up in the nasty quagmire of bossing each other around: Pass the butter; turn off the lights; pick up the dog food on your way home. No one should be spoken to that way.

In saying "Please" we unconsciously acknowledge one of the great gifts of being in love: the presence of the other person in our lives. We are grateful that she is there to assist us, that he desires to help us, that we treasure her enough to honor her by saying please.

Saying "Please" is also a way of respecting the person you love, of acknowledging that the things he or she gives and does aren't always the easiest or most fun to deliver. It is the implicit awareness that no matter how long you've been together, how much you love one another, or how much you feel free to ask or expect from each other, you always begin from the place of knowing that even the littlest labor of love requires a loving effort.

Saying "Please" is a way of always holding your beloved in high regard, of treating him or her as a person who still—and always—deserves to be approached with the graciousness that good manners confer. It's like polishing the silver. It gives the depth of reflection and kindness to your love, the luster of graciousness to even the most familiar gestures.

GIVE MORE GIFTS

Gifts lift our spirits and brighten our hearts by making us feel indulged and special, by making us feel worthy of the delightfully irrational pleasures of life. Although we know that at its highest, love is a mystical, spiritual union, it is in the daily, material world that we live and have our emotions, so gifts give us a sense of hope and joy about being alive.

Gifts make love concrete. Not only are they talismans of the special occasions of love—the engagement ring, the birthday watch, the anniversary necklace—but they are a material testament to the love of the giver and the preciousness of the receiver. When you're wearing the adorable tee shirt with the heart painted on it to your aerobics class, you can't help but remember that he really loves you. When you're carrying the stunning new attaché case she bought you for your birthday, you can't help but remember she thinks you're fabulous.

So do give more presents. Don't wait for special occasions. Buy the unnecessary, foolish, touching thing, the gift they says I love you, I know who you are. Be silly, be serious, be generous, be inventive: the china box with the pink ceramic bow, the fuzzy teddy bear, the gym bag with five pairs of tennis socks, the space age thermos, the porcelain thimble.

It doesn't have to be expensive—Denise picks up a few five

cent chocolates for her sweet-toothed husband on a semi-regular basis; he's always delighted. And it doesn't even have to be material. Giving each other the gift of time—to take a bubble bath without kids interrupting, play a round of golf, sleep in late—is a wonderful, rare present in this time-pressed day and age. It doesn't matter what it is. What matters is that you think of it and that, with a heart full of love, you give it.

If for some reason you have trouble giving or getting presents, perhaps when you were little you didn't receive the fits and treats you needed and now it's so painful to remember your disappointments that you'd rather dispense with gifts altogether. Maybe there was someone in your life whom you could never please, and now it's too scary to try to pick the right gift for the person you love. Or perhaps no one showed you how to receive or give gifts. Whatever the reason, you're missing out on something wonderful, a chance to brighten your spirits. So if you're shy about gifts, have a conversation with your sweetie about what hurts or makes it difficult—that'll be a gift in itself.

Not all of us, however, have trouble in this department. If you are already a champion present-giver, indulge your natural talent. No matter who you are, start now to enhance your relationship by giving more gifts.

ASK IF YOU CAN HELP

We are all sufficiently occupied with the things we do for our-selves and the things we have no choice about doing for our jobs, spouses, and/or children, that we don't necessarily have the time or inclination to do anything additional. Without helping anyone else, we have more than enough to keep us busy. That's why offering to help is a form of emotional graciousness that can add a lovely patina to your relationship.

Offering to help is more than just being willing to divide up the burden of the chores. It is a way of saying that, for no reason other than love, you are willing to enter into your sweetheart's undertakings. "Honey, I see you've been up all night doing the taxes; is there any way I can help you this morning?" "Do you need some help with the groceries"; "Your cold's getting worse; would you like me to get you some cough medicine"; "You sound really blue; would you like to talk to me about it?"

Help can come in many forms. It can be verbal solace (telling your honey everything is going to be all right), physical deliver-ance (lending a hand with the dishes), emotional comfort, (listen-ing to your sweetheart's woes), and a kind of jack-of-all trades willingness to do whatever is needed (is there anything at all that I can do for you?).

Offering to help says that we want our beloved's life to be

comfortable and gracious and we're willing to expend some energy to make it so. More than that, by offering to help, we acknowledge that we're not living in a vacuum, that we're not just born into the world to sit around and be waited on like Old King Cole. The world is not our oyster; our sweetheart is not our slave.

Offering to help is also an act of loving awareness. It says that, minute by minute, we specifically notice what's going on with the person we love and that we are willing to participate in his or her circumstances even at a very mundane level. This endears you to your love because, in a multitude of tiny, subliminal ways, he knows you're paying attention, she knows that you care. It's another way of affirming your connection, of saying you see yourself not as an island, but as part of the mainland created by your love.

She: "What are you thinking about right now?"

He: "Work."

She: "What about work?"

He: "My boss. He's been sick. He's been out for a week and the doctors haven't figured out what's wrong with him. I think he's got cancer and I'm scared. Work kills you—that's what I'm thinking about."

As this example shows, you can ask a ridiculous question and find out something profound. That's why I suggest that from time to time, you ask your love the silly question, and one with the obvious answer, the one you think you already know the answer to, the one that isn't worth asking in the first place, the one you're embarrassed to ask or afraid he or she will be too embarrassed to answer.

What's your favorite color? Were you happy when you were a kid? What are you thinking about right now? Why do you love me? Do you like your work? What do you want to be when you grow up? What's your secret dream? What do you need to do before you die? What turns you on? What do you like about your body?

When we fall in love, because of the power of our feelings for the other person—the lust, the excitement, the joy, the delight—we tend to presume that we know all about him, what makes him tick, what's important to her, what she thinks or feels at any given moment. This is a trap we can easily fall into, especially as time goes by. We spend so much time with this other person that we presume we know everything. But when we behave like know-it-alls, we miss a chance to surprise ourselves by discovering what we didn't know was there.

That's why you should ask the ridiculous question. Because it often leads to the very surprising answer, to a new discovery of the depth, complexity, and uniqueness of the person you love. To ask it is to invite yourself even more deeply into the knowing of another person. And truly knowing another person in all his or her endless big and little particulars—thoughts, feelings, intentions, disappointments, inadequacies, prayers, hopes, and sorrows—*is* love.

LISTEN FOR THE MEANING
BENEATH THE WORDS

At a recent party, a friend walked in late and I went over to give her a hug. I could feel that she didn't really receive it. She started talking in an offhanded way about being late—she had had to visit her brother, who was in the hospital. "Where are the hors d'ouerves?" she asked. "I'm starving." I put my hand on her arm, looked her straight in the eye and said, "You don't have to be so brave." Leaning her head on my shoulder, she cried, "I'm so scared he's not going to make it," and started bawling like a child.

What we say is often not what we mean. Our true feelings are frequently hidden in the intricate secret spaces between the words we utter. Most of us don't have the language to put the full extent of our feelings into words and lots of times we're not even sure what we're feeling anyway. For most of us, expressing our feelings precisely—especially when what we're feeling is sorrow, vulnerability, or shame—is extremely difficult. In the presence of such emotions, our words are often pitifully inaccurate, and what we reveal with our eyes and bodies is a much truer representation of our real message.

Therefore, when love listens, it listens with an ear and a heart to the unspoken. When you listen to your sweetheart, attend also to what he or she is not saying in words, for the meanings being expressed through the twitching finger, the heaving chest, the furrowed brow, the tear-clouded eye.

When you listen for the message under the words, you are listening with a feeling consciousness. From this place you can try to reach in with words of your own to touch the depths of the other person. Perhaps you can ask a very tender question: "You say you're happy but your eyes look sad. Would you like to tell me about it?" An open, inviting question can make your loved one feel safe enough to talk, and as your conversation moves delicately forward, the two of you can open the ground to a much deeper knowing, the knowing that comes from having heard the unspoken.

Walk a Mile in Your
Sweetheart's Shoes

One of the great pitfalls in a relationship is to use the other person as the handy-dandy dartboard for all the things that are bugging you. You can easily fall into the habit of blaming him for everything that goes wrong and/or expecting her to make everything right.

In order to avoid succumbing to this creepy possibility, try walking a mile in your sweetheart's shoes. Walking a mile in your sweetheart's shoes means that you will put yourself in her place, allow his experience to penetrate your consciousness, and feel it deeply enough so that you can console one another if necessary and not blame each other if tempted.

So, anytime you're sure he or she is at fault for your bad mood, the broken computer, the leak in the roof, the fact that life is boring, try putting yourself in his or her place. Imagine you are her and bring to mind the myriad stresses, insults, assaults, disappointments, and disasters, mini and gigantic, that are currently besetting her life. Take a minute to think about what traumas your partner is going through right now.

If you have trouble identifying with what your partner is feeling, if his boots are too big or her glass slipper only has room for your big toe, here's an exercise to try: Become your sweetheart.

Begin by saying, "I am _____," and call yourself by your sweetheart's name. Then, pretending you are him or her, start talking about what's going with "you." What's upsetting or delighting you right now? What has bruised or dampened your spirits? Try to see from inside his or her consciousness how your own critical, unsupportive, or blaming behavior feels when you are the person who has to receive it. What do you wish the person who loves you could do to understand or console you?

This is a very useful and often deeply moving exercise, especially when the two of you are at an emotional impasse. It's an opportunity for learning empathy from the inside by experiencing your own behavior through the other person's consciousness as you assume for a moment his or her emotional identity. "Being" her or him can move you very readily to a point of compassion that inevitably clears the way for more understanding between you.

To walk a mile in your sweetheart's shoes is to be able to see around the corner of your own assumptions, to see that in our need to be loved and understood, we are all one.

Say Thank You

Whatever is given to you, in whatever form it comes—praise, cash, kisses, compliments, candy, time, listening, lovemaking, letters, a new hat, a new house, a new car, a new baby, a planned vacation, a surprise vacation, an insight, a sense of security, a bouquet, the sharing of some feeling—say "Thank You."

Saying "Thank You" has a great effect on both partners. For the person being thanked, a thank you is a mirror of the love he or she has given. It not only increases our sense of ourselves as loving persons, but enlarges our capacity to be loving. Of course we don't give something just to get thanked, but getting thanked allows us to see the value of what we have been given and makes us willing to give again.

Saying "Thank You" is also important for the person who says it. On the simplest level, it's an act of courtesy, a recognition of the good thing the other person has done. But on a much deeper level, it's a way of changing our consciousness about the nature of our relationships. For, in uttering our gratitude, we anchor in our minds the fact that we've been given to and are cherished.

It's all too easy, in any relationship, to become (internally at least) a whining, complaining grump who feels as if the other person has never done, and will never do, anything nice or special for you. Saying "Thank You" dispels this feeling of hopelessness and creates an internal attitude of optimism. A pathway is formed in our minds which in time becomes a thoroughfare; the belief that we have been treated with generosity and goodness of heart, that we have, if you will, been loved, begins to take root in our consciousness. In this sense saying "Thank You" is a character-building act. It develops a positive view of the person we love, and also of the world.

Just as millions of snowflakes pile up to create a blanket of snow, the "Thank You's" we say pile up and fall gently upon one another until in our hearts and minds we are adrift in gratitude.

Treasuring Your Relationship

PUT YOUR LOVE ON A BILLBOARD

Pamela and Don, who'd been married for years, were out to dinner with some of Don's business associates, including a newlywed couple. In congratulating the two on their marriage, Don said, "I'm so happy for you because marriage has been so wonderful for me. Pamela's so intelligent and beautiful and witty. She believes in me when I try; she comforts me when I fail; I always know she loves me—and she gets my jokes. That's why she's the perfect woman for me."

"That means more to me than all the things you've ever said in private," Pamela responded, and their exchange became a celebration for the two of them and an inspiration for their tablemates.

Putting your love on a billboard is the opposite of acting as if your relationship should be one of the best-kept secrets in the Western world. Instead of hiding your relationship under a bushel, you hold it up like a banner for everyone to see.

We tend to think that keeping a lid on our love is the socially correct thing to do. It's as if we have a social contract that says "in private we love; in public we act like civilized strangers." The truth is nothing makes us feel better than to be lauded in public or to experience in company the fact that our mate thinks our relationship is worth crowing over. It's as if by seeing our relationship or spouse through the eyes of others, we're allowed to discover from a slightly different perspective what a wonderful treasure it is.

I'm not talking here about making a passionate public spectacle of your romance; simply about honoring it publicly, letting the people who form the social fabric of your life know that your love is precious to you, that it fills your heart and gives meaning to your life.

Putting your love on a billboard goes beyond the perfunctory "I'd like to thank my lovely wife," or "Without the continued support of my husband," and reaches into the realm of deeply felt and specific acknowledgement. It gives the partner you are celebrating a deliciously puffed-up thrill to be so celebrated, and gives the people who hear your testimonial a sense of hope about the power of love.

So no matter how long you have been together, honor one another in front of strangers and friends. Warm feelings will multiply when you make a beautiful example of your love.

Commiserate with One Another

To commiserate means to be in misery with. Commiseration isn't about solving problems; it is bearing loving witness to life's small and large insolubles. In a relationship, it's the chance to share your experience of the slings an arrows of daily life, and to know that you can both tell your troubles and give the gift of smoothing out your partner's ruffled feathers.

Alice had a way of unloading her troubles without much prompting. She used to let Francis have it all the minute he walked in the door—how she had been stalled for 45 minutes on the freeway, how the computer broke down at work so she couldn't get her project out on time, how the grocery check-out line was six miles long. One day, after he had consoled her, she noticed the gap of silence that followed her recitation and found herself feeling a little embarrassed. "Don't you have any troubles?" she asked finally.

"Of course," he said, taken aback.

"Well, why don't you ever tell me about them?" she asked.

"I guess I never thought to. Or I thought I never could. It seemed to me like our deal was that you were supposed to complain and I was supposed to sympathize."

All too often when it comes to commiseration, as with Alice and Francis until they caught themselves, couples tend to artificially polarize so that one partner becomes the complainer and the other the sounding board and consoler. But co-miseration means just that—a joint venture in the sharing of the insulting trouncings of life.

Commiserating is important because life is rife with assaults and insults, which, if we don't unload them as they occur, will clump together, crumple our spirits, and get expressed in some inappropriate, sideways fashion that can cause real trouble. It's like the old cliché about the man who gets yelled at by his boss and comes home and kicks the dog. All too often it's the niggling, piddling things that bother us which, uncommiserated with, can lead us to inappropriately attacking our sweethearts.

It's important to remember that things and people outside the protected circle of your happy union can have a great effect on it. Rather than imagining that you can handle these little insults and disappointments alone, bring them to the table of your relationship, express them, receive the balm of consolation, and then let them go. This way you can have love in your relationship instead of the misplaced anger that can collect from the trials of daily life. After all, if we can't commiserate about the little stuff, how will we ever console one another about life's tragedies?

Negotiate the Mundane

The trouble with life is that it's so daily. Sooner or later, every relationship comes down to who's going to take out the trash.

Facing that any relationship includes what at times can feel like a seemingly endless amount of chores is one of the higher duties of love. For it acknowledges that love, an experience of transcendence, occurs in the mundane, material world. Accepting this is in itself an act of love, for it means that for the cause of love, we will humble ourselves to do all manner of boring and annoying tasks graciously.

One of the dangers of the daily nature of life is that we may be inclined to see these chores as being a consequence of our relationships and not of life itself. It's a great temptation to blame the other person for the ickiness of ordinary life, as if, if we were alone, we wouldn't have to make the bed, do laundry, deal with the exploding water heater, or fix the ailing car. It's also easy to get unreasonable and picky about neglected tasks or our partner's chores we sometimes end up doing. However, our responsibility in love is not to expect that such trivialities will disappear nor that just for love the other person (or we ourselves) will unflinchingly do everything. Rather, real love knows that the dishes need to be done and is willing to negotiate about it. True love is grateful that the burden can be shared. This means talking about it, figuring out who's going to do what, making a list, and not expecting that elves will come along and do it all. Negotiation also requires compromise—for example, accepting, without complaint, that the other person might not clean the toilet bowl as perfectly as you would, or being willing to do certain tasks, like washing his filthy work jeans, that you wouldn't do if you were living alone.

Negotiating the mundane means that you accept the dish pans and trash cans of life and decide together how chores are going to be done. Then, instead of being bones of contention, and the most significant things in life, chores can recede into the background so you can do the really important things—like discovering your destiny and making love.

ACKNOWLEDGE THE HARDSHIPS YOUR CIRCUMSTANCES CREATE

Just being ourselves creates burdens for our loved ones. No matter who we are—a movie star, a mother of five who's married for the second time, a graduate student, a diabetic, or someone with an upside-down work schedule—we've all arrived at our relationships dragging along the barnacles of circumstances that, at times, make us difficult to love. Stepchildren, ailing parents, broken cars, wacky sisters—we all have conditions that make loving us a hardship for the person who has chosen to love us.

The sad truth is that most of us have too many obligations and too little time. We don't mean to drive our spouses crazy by having to attend ten late night meetings in a row, by having 20 outfits strewn across the bedroom floor because we haven't had time to pick them up, by having a toothache six days running—but we do. In these and a myriad of other ways, we unintentionally abuse one another. We all require too much from one another; in a sense, we're all asking each other to do the impossible all the time.

Love makes our partners willing to put up with all this real life nonsense, but the truth is that we need to be mindful of, grateful for, and apologetic about the hardships our circumstances cause. It's easy to react from defensiveness or guilt by thinking or saying, "Putting up with my sick mother can't be all that bad," or "He shouldn't complain about how much I have to work."

But we really do need to own up to all these things. Remembering how we stretch one another, and saying the appropriate "Please bear with me," "Thank you for putting up with my insane schedule," or simply "I'm sorry," will create, in the midst of these taxing situations, moments in which we can appreciate the inordinate generosity and forbearance of one another. Rather than irritants that become divisive and destructive, our hardships become occasions for deepening intimacy. Acknowledging what we inflict and require makes it possible for our mates to endure the unendurable, and forges a new connection of love between us.

KEEP IN TOUCH

In these days of inordinately busy and complex schedules, it is actually possible to lose touch with the person you love, sometimes for days at a time. That's why we need to make an effort to keep a hand on not only the pulse of our obligations and plans, but also on the heartbeat of our intimate relationships.

Keeping in touch means that you will keep your partner thoughtfully apprised of your life and times—your schedule, and obligations, as well as variations in routines and plans. There's nothing worse, for example, than having a sick child and being unable to track down your mate. Or being told he'll arrive at six p.m., only to have him show up two hours later. Or setting aside a weekend to be together only to be informed at the last minute that she can only spare Sunday from two to four. Of course, emergencies and exceptions come up, but having the commitment to fill one another in as much as possible, as soon as possible, will give your honey the resilience to withstand the irritating exceptions.

But keeping in touch should be more than merely a exchange of scheduling information. It also means that you'll find ways to communicate your love on a regular basis, regardless of how busy you are. In this way you keep telling sweetheart that it's him you want to come home to, that it's her you adore.

One couple I know keeps a book on the living room table.

When either of them has to be gone, he or she never goes away without leaving a message of love for the other person. They've been married eight years and the book is the heartfelt tracing of a daily life lived out in thoughtfulness and love.

A woman who travels a lot for business never goes out of town without leaving a special love note for her husband propped up on his pillow. And he never welcomes her home from one of these jaunts without having arranged a bouquet of flowers for her by the bed.

Another woman has a spot on the back door jamb where she leaves a welcome home note for her sweetheart. A man whose work takes him out of the country for weeks at a time sends a postcard home every day. It always says the same thing: "I would be having a wonderful time—if only you were here." Another man, a busy attorney, calls home every day to say "Have I told you today that I love you?" These seemingly little gestures can make all the difference to our hearts in an obligation-hobbled world.

Keeping in touch is the antidote to taking for granted. It means that you treat your lover as special, and is a way of reminding yourself that your love is special too.

TAKE INTIMATE TIME

All too often we treat our relationships as if they were cars that could run without gasoline. We expect them to look good, keep us safe inside, give us a self-image, and get us where we are going—all without even the basic maintenance.

Don't let your relationship run out of gas. Intimate time is the fuel of a fine relationship. Taking the time means that rather than expecting your relationship simply to provide you with all the benefits you want—sex, companionship, emotional solace, parenting of children, financial security—you understand that a relationship needs the sustenance of shared private thoughts and feelings, and you make a commitment to find the time.

Intimate time can run the gamut from the "five-minute check in" at a set time (the breakfast or dinner table, just before sleep) that covers the bases of information about your day, to a daily reunion of 20 minutes or more when you each have time to reveal yourself on a more intricate level. Here you can talk more thoroughly with one another, revealing your fears, your goals, your ongoing intentions and daily frustrations, your joys. This is when you can share your hurts and disappointments (both those you have caused each other and those inflicted by the outside world), encourage one another, and make plans.

Taking intimate time also means creating opportunities for the other sweet intimacies of love: a walk on the beach or around the block in the snow; a hide-away weekend in the desert or the mountains or simply at the Motel 6 around the corner. It also means creating the chance to make love leisurely, to spend a whole day in bed, curl up together on the couch, kiss more than perfunctorily, hold hands across the dinner table.

Frankly, I believe if you can't find 20 or 30 minutes a day for some kind of intimate encounter, your relationship is a toboggan on a downhill run toward a big black rock. Taking intimate time for your love means that instead of depriving your relationship of the sweet essentials it needs, you will be generous in finding time for them.

KINDLE THE ROMANCE

Romance is the champagne and frosted glasses of love, the magic that gives love a tango to dance to, a fragrance to remember, and a fantasy-come-true to hold in your heart. Romance is the antidote to ordinariness, the inspiration for passion; whenever you fold it into your relationship, you instantly elevate it to a more delicious state of being. Romanced, you feel beautiful or handsome; life becomes ripe with hope; the moon, stars, and planets bathe you in a cascade of beneficent light; and you believe everything is possible—your sweetest, wildest, and most cherished dreams will certainly come true.

At least that's certainly how we feel in the rosy blush of new romance. But the feeling of romance doesn't just stick around all by itself. As time goes on, it takes effort, ingenuity, intuition, and sometimes even a willingness to feel foolish, to keep the moonlight magical. That's because somewhere along the line, without quite paying attention, we stop doing the things that kindled romance in the first place: we forget to bring the long-stemmed roses, and to whisper the sweet nothings; we leave the lights on (or off), we trade in the black lingerie for flannel pajamas. In short, we start treating one another as roommates instead of passionate lovers.

But we can all still have romance in our lives, no matter how long we've been together. Chill the glasses. Remember the roses. Install the new dimmer, light the candles and forget about the wax drip-dripping on the table, play the song you first heard on your honeymoon. Dress the bed in red sheets. Drive up the hill to watch the sunset and kiss (and kiss) in the car.

Every so often Paul plays a romantic SOS trick on Sonja. He calls her up from somewhere, says he's having trouble with his car, and asks if she can please come pick him up. When she arrives, it turns out he's "stranded" near some hotel. He hands her a beautifully wrapped present—a dress or a sexy new nightgown. He checked them into a room and orders dinner from room service. After dinner they go dancing and then make passionate love.

When it comes to kindling romance, you have to be willing to be creative, even if at first you feel shy or embarrassed. Remember, you weren't embarrassed by all those love notes and love songs when you were falling in love. The art of romance takes practice. The more you allow yourself to stretch the limits of what feels comfortable to you, the more inventive you'll become, especially if your initial efforts garner a positive response. (And if you're the receiver of these endeavors to enchant, be sure to respond. If you do you'll increase the romance quotient in your life.)

Whatever your particular romantic preferences may be, be sure to indulge them as much as you can. Don't let opportunities slip through the cracks. Like the love it will embellish, romance is a very special art form whose reward is the joy of passion.

WATCH YOUR TONGUE

After years of his wife Janna's steadfast labor and infinite patience helping him do research and typing his doctoral dissertation, John carelessly said to her in a fight, "Who needs you anyway? You've never done a thing for me." Janna was crushed. She told me afterwards she felt as if a bomb had gone off inside her. She went to the bedroom, took out a suitcase, packed some clothes, and moved into a motel. It took months of negotiations and therapy before she and John reconciled.

The moral of the story? Be careful what you say. Just because you're upset and get carried away in a fight is no excuse to assassinate your loved one's character. Sticks and stones may break your ones, but words always have the potential of creating deep and sometimes even irreversible hurts. Comments about a person's intelligence, body, value, or ability to love (to say nothing of comparisons with past lovers, sweethearts, or spouses) can, in fact, shake your mate to the core. We don't like to think that something said in anger could have a lasting effect, but it can. Nasty remarks can be so devastating as to permanently mar the self-esteem of the other person or irrevocably damage the goodwill of your relationship.

So avoid the gratuitous mean-spirited remark: "Well you can just go get a divorce then"; "I'm leaving"; "You never loved me anyway"; "I hate your kids"; "I hate this house"; "I hate my life"; "You've never understood me"; ""You're too fat"; "I think I'll go find Mr. Perfect. He'll realize how wonderful I am"; "I'm going back to Susie Q. At least she knew how to make love."

A relationship always sinks to its lowest common denominator, so when you allow yourself to indulge in such spirit-violating attacks, you immediately bring the relationship down to a tit-for-tat level that at the very least dumps a load of garbage on the path to real communication and can potentially leave your relationship in ruins.

Whether we know it or not, we all have a kind of cruel sixth sense about the words that can really devastate our partners. We all know the sensitive, vulnerable place, the spiritual Achilles heel in which he or she can be mortally bruised. That's why we need to watch our tongues. Think twice or a dozen times, count to ten or ten hundred, before you say the thing that could be totally devastating.

Depart and Reunite with Loving Gestures

Remember how, when you were falling in love, you couldn't wait to see one another, couldn't wait to hold his hand, to kiss her lips? And how leaving one another was pure torture, a heartbreak to be postponed as long as possible? Just because the fires of new romance have become the steady embers of real love doesn't mean you don't still need the blessing of coming together and departing with loving rituals.

By coming together with loving welcome, we acknowledge that we are re-entering the presence and spirit of the person we love, and that we do so happily. By departing with a special farewell, we put a loving seal on one another, showing that we don't take one another for granted.

So if you are going away on a business trip, don't just pack your bags and disappear. Be sure to take your loved one into your arms and say that you'll miss him or her. When you walk in the door, put down your briefcase, and stop to kiss your partner. Don't just waltz in with an "I'm home" and head for the den or the mail. And if you're home first, don't just lie on the couch glued to the TV, without so much as a word of hello. Stop what you're doing, make contact, kiss, embrace, look into one another's eyes, take in each other's soul.

And don't open the exchange of your reuniting with a "What

took you so long?" "Where the hell have you been?" or "Why isn't dinner ready?" Before you get on with the facts and demands of real life, STOP and acknowledge the person with whom you have chosen to share your life.

We need to do this to remind ourselves that it is love, above all, that binds us; that it is love which remains when the workaday world is over. It is to love that we return. Even when we are unable to bask in a long or deep experience of lovingness, the kisses and embraces of greeting and departure are the vivid symbols of what our hearts intend, of our wish to be together long and lovingly.

If all this hugging and kissing seems silly, remember that we never really know, do we, that we will see one another again. So even the smallest reunion is a tiny miracle.

FIGHT THE GOOD FIGHT

No relationship is without conflict—differences of opinion, preference, and even direction—and a relationship is only as good as the conflict it can contain. By this I mean that a relationship has vitality only to the degree that it can endure the stresses of individual differences and resolve them through healthy conflict so that the relationship and the individuals in it can move toward greater authenticity.

Many of us are scared of conflict because we don't know how to fight. We're afraid our own anger will run away with us, that we will lose control and become vicious, vituperative, or even physically destructive. We're also afraid of the other person's anger—will he or she yell, throw things, slam the door, walk out? These behaviors can sometimes occur and can even be a real danger, especially for people who have been abused with anger themselves. But even they can learn to express anger in a constructive way.

The sign of a good fight is that it makes you both feel you have discovered something, that you know one another better. Even if you fight again and again about the same issues (and most of us do), a good fight gives you hope about the future because you have gained a measure of insight about something that previously baffled or frustrated you.

Here's some help: 1. Try to see what you are angry about. This is usually something very specific: "That you didn't call," not "Because life is miserable." 2. State your feeling and why you feel that way: "I'm angry that you didn't call because it makes me feel unloved." 3. Say what you need in recompense: "I need you to apologize." 4. After your mate has given the apology, ask yourself and him or her if you feel totally resolved. 5. Kiss and make up.

For example, "I'm angry at you for yelling at me about burning the tea kettle. You embarrassed me in front of Kay. It made me feel belittled to have her hear you talk to me like that. I need you to apologize." "I'm sorry, honey. I was in such a rush this morning and was anxious about that big meeting. I was out of line. I don't want to make you feel that way. Please forgive me."

This, of course, would win the Academy Award for Most Civilized Fight, and with your high feelings and sense of frustration over the number of times the hateful thing has happened, to say nothing of your just plain humanness, you probably won't always be able to muster quite so much graciousness. In any case, try to remember: 1. A good fight isn't a free-for-all. Don't say everything you feel like saying even though you may have a legitimate gripe. Remember that words can wound, and after the fight you don't want a battered mate. 2. Be specific with your complaints. Don't throw in all your grievances since time began. 3. Let the other person's words sink in before you take up your cudgel. Remember you're having this fight to learn something, to arrive at some new insight as well as an immediate resolution. 4. Go easy on yourself and your honey when you don't do it perfectly.

LEAVE THE KITCHEN SINK IN THE KITCHEN

When fighting, leave the kitchen sink in the kitchen. What I mean by this is don't just gratuitously throw in things that don't belong in the current fight—every complaint you've had since the history of time began, something corroded and calcified from 16 years ago, or the meanest, below-the-belt thing that you can possibly think of saying.

Kitchen sink behavior isn't profitable. It doesn't do anything except fan the flames of contention, and open an abyss of panic and pain your mate. Once you've gotten the satisfaction of watching the sink fly by and crash into the wall, you may have a hard time cleaning up after yourself.

So no matter what you're so furious about, try to resist the temptation to let it all hang out or to let the devil take the hindmost. It's important to stop and think before you let the other person have it. Ask yourself two questions:

1. *Do I really need to say this?* That is, does this horrible, angry, vituperative, or character-blasting thing really need to be said? Will it improve the immediate situation? Is there anything useful to be gained from saying, for example, that you not only think your sex life is awful now, but

it has been for the past ten years? Will this or similar remarks speed up the other person's evolution, or your own, or is saying it just the indulgence of revved-up emotions that want release?

2. *Do I really need to say this NOW?* The diatribe you want to indulge in may include some very valuable points that really do need to be expressed. But is this the time to make them? Will you set off a furor or engender a useful response?

Before we fire our verbal machine guns it's important that we investigate the maturity of our emotional output and consider that just because we feel like saying something doesn't necessarily mean it needs to be said in the way or at the moment we feel like saying it. Remember your relationship is a precious thing that deserves to be preserved, and look for a more appropriate time and way to express your feelings so that your relationship will be enhanced, and not eroded.

REMEMBER THE EARLY DAYS
OF YOUR LOVE

In the bash and crash of daily life, it's very easy indeed to forget why we love one another: she's come home late for the sixth night in a row, he's been short-tempered and surly again, nobody's said anything sweet for what seems like ten weeks. It's at times like these that we need to remember the romantic days of falling in love.

In order to nourish and refresh your relationship, you need to remind yourself from time to time about the happy hours of your early love. Every love has the ravishing early moments of romance—the sunset walk along the pier, the tear-washed face of goodbye at the international airport, the stolen kisses when your love was still a secret. It was what you experienced in these moments that you need to remember and share.

"I saw her walking in the garden at the house where I was visiting, and her movements so totally enchanted me I knew I had to marry her. I just wanted to be able to watch her forever."

"He asked me to go on a hike. We started up the mountain and I turned my ankle and started to fall. But instantly he caught me. 'Gotcha,' he said, and I fell back into his arms and felt totally protected. I could sense his great kindness and thought to myself, 'He's a wonderful man—I'm falling in love.'"

Just talking together about these memories can revive those wonderful feelings, especially if you do it in such a way that it brings you together, and not in a blaming "remember-how-you-kissed-me-500-times-a-day-and-now-you-never-do" way. Whatever it was that made you fall in love, remembering it will give you the stamina and generosity of spirit to go on, a way to feel that, "Oh yes, there *is* a good reason to put up with all of this."

Love that grows threadbare and dingy with time can be instantly revived by the memory of what was magic to both of you at the outset. Whatever bonded you initially was real and powerful, and you can lose sight of that as time goes on. When you allow yourself to remember your falling in love, you make the things that brought you together as strong as the things that are undermining your relationship at the moment.

So remember why you fell in love and the magic will happen again.

Be Willing to Make
the Generous Gesture

Especially in fights where angry fevers are already running high, we all have a tendency to get stubborn, to bullishly hold our positions, and to be damned if we'll back down.

In any relationship longer than three weeks old there are probably grounds for divorce. One way or another we all do millions of things that bother, irritate, violate, and break the heart of one another. All isn't fair in love and war, and what I mean by this is that the abuses of both love and war are endless, and we'd better not try to delude ourselves into thinking otherwise.

It's because love has the capacity to infinitely wound us, that, when we're in a tough spot with the person we love, we can feel as if we've gone miles beyond our limits and that, in order to preserve our dignity, our sanity, and our skin, we absolutely must not back down, give up, or give in.

Stubbornness does serve as self-preservation, and rightly so, for we shouldn't stand for the kind of mistreatment that is actually abuse. But it can also stand in the way of progress if we refuse to back down even when, for the sake of the union, we should. When we're feeling ripped off, taken advantage of, or ignored, impasses such as "I'm right," "No, I'm right"; "Be nice to me," "Not until you be nice to me first"; "It's all your fault," "What do you mean?—It's all

YOUR fault," can send your relationship into a brutally plummeting downward spiral from which it may never recover.

A stalemate isn't a very creative place. Nothing can be accomplished, forgiven, resolved, or revised when we stand head to head refusing to budge. We can't expect progress unless one of the two billy goats butting heads takes the first step to unlocking horns.

Therefore, be willing to say "Ok, I'll back off and really try to listen to you this time." For the really stubborn at heart, here's a trick: Say "I'll be nice if you'll be nice," then, on the count of three, start talking again at the place where you were before you both got so stubborn.

True love flourishes in the air of compassion. The gesture that bridges the gap of abuse, exhaustion, and disappointment is the emotionally heroic act. Be willing to be a hero in your relationship by going beyond your limits to make the generous gesture, the gesture that will nourish and preserve your union.

Accentuate the Positive

Accentuating the positive means you will choose the best way to interpret what the other person is saying or doing. It's easy, when you're emotionally intimate, to start getting scared—that love won't last, that your dreams will get broken, that things aren't as good as you hoped, that the other person will leave, that you've been fooled, that you're being taken advantage of.

While disappointment is possible in even the best of relationships (nobody's perfect, remember), what is more often true is that we have come together in good will, with every hope and intention of having things work out as wonderfully as possible for everyone involved. In other words, the person you love is not out to get you.

Remembering this in the midst of the hairy frays and unavoidable little conflicts of love insures that your relationship won't plummet into a downward spiral of negativity. When you emphasize the negative, "I know you don't love me"; "I know you did that just to bug me"; "I know you don't care how I feel"; "I know this will never work out"; "I know you loved her more than you'll ever love me," you elevate it to the realm of ever higher possibility.

When you accentuate the positive, you start form the position that the mistake wasn't caused by your partner's obnoxious personality, incompetence, or vile intentions to assault, insult, attack, disappoint, or otherwise alienate you. You allow yourself and your partner a chance to feel good, to improve the situation. Instead of "You always try to confuse me," try "I'm sorry, honey, I guess I didn't quite understand what you were saying. Could you please explain it again?" Instead of "Why are you talking so weird to me," try "Your voice sounds a little off. Are you ok?"

We all make mistakes. We all have circumstances. There are a million and one reasons why any particular behavior occurs (or doesn't occur) and why it appears the way it does to you. Before you assume the worst, imagine that the happiest, most optimistic, or good intentioned of all the options has occurred. Then take a deep breath, inquire, and wait for the explanation that may well dissolve all your fears and even arouse your compassion.

FLUFF UP THE EGO OF YOUR LOVE

Just when you're stranded at an airport waiting for the plane that's six hours late you feel as if you've always been stuck in the airport, so when you're in the midst of some sort of relationship fracas, it's easy to feel that conflict and upset are all that have ever occurred, or are ever going to, within the portals of your intimate relationship.

In truth, most of our loves serve us well. Even in the hardest of times they dispense the lessons we most need to learn, and in the best of times they deliver us to the joys we most desire.

Fluffing up the ego of your relationship is reminding yourself and your beloved of all the good things your relationship represents. It is consciously keeping track of all the wonderful things you do, have done, will do, and have become together. Fluffing up the ego of your relationship is understanding that there is a state of the union that deserves recognition.

For example, you may have stopped noticing what a beautiful couple you are. Other people still notice but by now you take it for granted. Beginning now, start remembering what a pleasure it is to share your life with a person whose personal style so perfectly complements yours. Or maybe you've forgotten that you really are incredibly well matched intellectually. Who else could you have those free-wheeling, mind-roving conversations with; who else knows the meaning of *antepenultimate* or could remember the elevation of Macchu Pichu?

Remember again how truly supportive you are of each other, how you really do stick up for one another when the chips are down, when he doesn't get chosen for the baseball team, when her paintings are rejected for the juried show.

When you fluff up the ego of your love, you make every effort to note that something more than your individual selves has been created in your coming together. "We have a lot of fun together, don't we?" "We've made a beautiful home here, haven't we?" "We've really got a great bunch of kids"; "I can't remember life before US. Now everything makes sense."

These kinds of acknowledgements have an amazingly positive effect. They allow you to hold your relationship in your consciousness as a source of strength and nurturance, a resource for your individual identities, a shield of protection as you go out into the world. Therefore, both in talking to yourself and to your beloved, acknowledge the goodness you have created in your union. Doing so will keep you connected to the power of your bondedness.

Tie Up Your Emotional Loose Ends

Emotional loose ends are those little hanging-on, nagging incompletenesses between you and your mate: unexpressed resentments, unbandaged hurts, unresolved conflicts, unmentioned little embarrassments, requests that are hiding in the background. Unsaid, they stand between you and your mate, spoiling your emotional bond, clouding the clarity you'd like to have with one another.

When you tie up emotional loose ends, instead of letting your conflicts, poignancies, and difficulties fester in the slough of non-expression, you bring them to a conclusion and make peace with one another before going on. Doing this implies that you both desire and believe you can bring your union to the place of emotional homeostasis, of calm, in which you can once again take the tender emotional risks that deepen a relationship.

A relationship needs a consistent, ground level of harmony, a safe place from which the people in it can take the chances that enhance their own growth and nurture the bonds that connect them. Tying up your emotional loose ends is a way of keeping this sanctuary clear.

We all have a tendency to let things go, to hope that whatever's amiss will just work itself out or disappear. Some things do become conveniently irrelevant in time, but the truth is that not resolving takes an incredible amount of energy. And all this energy could much better be used for kissing each other or making plans to go to the movies.

Yvonne was still mad at Claude about a fight they'd had on Friday. When they went out on Saturday night, instead of being able to relax and enjoy herself, she was cranky and unsettled. There was one thing he'd said—"I really don't like you talking on the phone with Laura (Yvonne's best friend) all the time"—that had particularly hurt her. She relied on the fun, diversion, and support of her frequent chats with Laura, and it was scary to think that Claude would have such a negative reaction. But instead of telling him about it, she "hoped he didn't really mean it," or that "he'd get over it." She even thought about making a snide remark about Ned, Claude's best friend, the next time the two of them went golfing. But none of these efforts to shove things under the rug had worked. Yvonne was still upset and not talking about it only had the effect of spoiling their Saturday night.

This is a perfect example of how emotional loose ends can turn into romantic nooses. So instead of building a gallows for your love, take the extra time and care to resolve your unfinished emotional business, no matter how trite or inconsequential it may seem. Love blossoms under blue skies, tying up emotional loose ends shoos all the clouds away.

APOLOGIZE, APOLOGIZE, APOLOGIZE

It's really very simple, but so very hard to do. When you make a mistake, apologize: "I'm sorry. You're right. I did forget to pick up the cleaning. Please forgive me." "I'm sorry I yelled. I know I scared you." "I'm sorry I wasn't listening. I do want to hear what you're saying."

Acknowledging both your flaws as a person and also your specific boo-boos—the small and big mistakes, the rotten little things you do or forget to do—is the great janitorial broom of a good relationship. It clears the debris from the path to your loved one's heart, a path that can all too easily get cluttered with nagging little resentments. Apologizing is a way of keeping current with your relationship, of making sure that the two of you aren't loving through a window so fogged by old complaints that it's impossible to see or be seen clearly by one another.

Apology consists of three essential parts: stating your crimes by name, saying you're sorry, and asking to be forgiven. It differs radically from defensiveness. When we are defensive, we become lawyers for our own case; "I did it because...," "I didn't mean to do it," "he, she or it made me do it," "It isn't what it appears to be," "It's all in your mind," "It was not big deal."

All these defensive postures have the effect of muddying the emotional waters. They obscure our true shortcomings, flaws, and mistakes, and require that we be loved at a shallow level—the level of self-deception—and not at the depth of our emotional integrity. When we own up to our mistakes, we ask that we be loved in the full measure of our humanness, imperfect though we may be.

Defensiveness is a way of keeping a relationship problem going. Apology gives closure, opening the path to forgiveness and a new beginning. Most of us can never apologize enough. Apology—when it is genuine and comes from the heart—is one of the quickest healers of any-sized rift, the perfect bandage for every wound in a relationship.

PLAY WITH ONE ANOTHER

When we play we feel the carefree joyfulness of our spirits. We are delivered from the bonds of obligation and responsibility to a sense of delight about ourselves. Playing allows us to rekindle the sense of the child in us, to go back to a time when life was new and full of possibility. Because inside we are all still young, we need to play as much as we can.

Playing alone or with others—a round of golf, an aerobics class, a soccer game, a tennis match—isn't just frivolous nonsense. Play creates balance. It's the safety net under the tightrope of modern life; it keeps us sane and functioning.

Playing alone is good. Playing together is better. Playing with the person you love is the premier form of play. Playing combines both the intrinsic joys of play with the opportunity to have a totally carefree experience (and sometimes mind-altering view) of the person you love. Seeing and being with him at his most spontaneous, at her most innocent and unguarded, can only deepen your appreciation of him, your sense of the specialness of her. For when we do what we love, we are most precisely ourselves.

Shared foolishness deepens bonds.

"Remember when we climbed the 500 steps up the sand dune and then when we got to the water tower it was all fenced in? We climbed up anyway and I ripped my shorts on the barbed wire fence. Wasn't that view incredible?"

"Remember when we held the croquet tournament over Labor Day and you won?" "Remember when we went to the MacIntoshes' Halloween party and I was a ballerina and you were a cat?" "Remember the summer we played badminton on the back lawn every single night after supper?"

Playing together—whether you play house, play yard, play sports, play dress-up-and-go-out—always doubles the fun because you feel not only the pleasure of your sweetheart's company, but also the pleasure of the thing you love to do.

Therefore, PLAY PLAY PLAY. Play well. Play hard. Play on. Play often. Play for keeps.

CELEBRATE WITH CEREMONIES

Love flourishes when it's shored up by the joy of celebration. Celebrations acknowledge special events: birthdays, anniversaries, promotions, awards, graduations—the cycles of our lives and loves. Celebrations are the fairy dust that ritualistically enlivens the commonplace continuum of daily life. They keep us in touch with, and make us take note of, the things that make our lives and loves precious.

We were all delighted by ceremonies when we were children—the tooth fairy, the Christmas stocking, the Easter Bunny, the pony rides at birthday parties. Just because we have outgrown our childhood britches doesn't mean we have outgrown our need for ceremony. Even though we may have become more self-conscious, we are still needy of such commemorative events in our lives.

It is these special moments, ritualized by their repetitiveness, that give us a sense of rootedness, that draw us close together. Indeed, it is the very fact that ceremony has a repetitive aspect that creates a certain portion of our enjoyment. We know that the magical things will unfold in exactly the same way as they have before and this in itself delights us.

Love needs the benediction of celebration and ceremony. Rick always gives Shelly a chocolate bunny for Easter. Suzanne and Rene always go back for their summer vacation to the cottage on the lake where Suzanne grew up. Mark and Marie always spend their anniversary at the hotel where one day 13 years ago, they first exchanged glances beside the pool.

Sara makes a nightshirt for Paul every Christmas and embroiders its pocket with a coat of arms. Each year when the new shirt appears, Paul cuts out the old insignia from last year's shirt and keeps it in a special box where, by now, he has more than a dozen tokens of her love.

Walter always orders a bakery birthday cake for Cerise, one with stand-up numbers like the ones she had on her cakes when she was a little girl in France. He always writes the same thing on her card: "So you'll feel younger while you're growing older."

So celebrate the special occasions in your life with your own personal ceremonies. Ceremonies order and embroider our intimate lives.

In the intimate circumstance, there aren't any extra points for being brave. Bravery is fakery, the antithesis of intimacy. Bravery is living a lie. In order to have a truly meaningful relationship, you need to be willing to talk about what you're afraid of.

For some reason, especially in the United States, we're all ashamed of being afraid. We're taught that fears are for sissies and that, when we finally "get it together," we will have transcended fear and can say, like Ernest Hemingway, that we're "'fraid a' nothin'."

The truth is that our fears refer to some very tender places in ourselves, areas where we've been hurt, where we haven't quite grown up, where we're not yet strong enough or have already had our fondest hopes smashed to bits. Our fears are as various as the petty fear of spiders or the fear of our own mortality. But no matter how inconsequential or overwhelming they may seem, they are reports from the fragile interiors of our psyches. In revealing them, we give our partners access to the points where we need to be nurtured; where, because of our vulnerabilities, we are most able to be loved.

Thus, unveiling your fears is an act of openness that counts on the loving response. It says, "I know that you love me enough to allow me to show you my weakness. I trust you to be careful with me." When we tell our honeys we're afraid, this trust in itself becomes a compliment to the beloved.

Disclosing your fears also brings you immediately to the level of greater intimacy, because one of our biggest fears is that the other person has it all together and we alone are the sole chicken-hearted idiot on the face of the earth. But revealing what you are afraid of usually prompts the other person to divulge his or her fears too. In this way exposing your fears puts you at once in alignment with the innermost self of the other person, with what he is afraid of, where she feels terrified and alone. And it is being together in the midst of our vulnerabilities that is the experience of bonding which is at the very heart of love.

SHARE YOUR DREAMS

Our dreams, whether the dreams we have at night or the hopes and aspirations we have for our lives, represent some of the most profound, protected, and precious parts of ourselves. Because they are so private, when we share them we immediately create intimacy.

Images from our sleep are a map of our unsuspected and uncensored selves. They are messages to us and about us from the deepest reaches of our unconscious. In the enigmatic language of our own private symbols, they reveal the secrets we keep even from ourselves.

Telling your sweetheart your dreams is an act of self-revelation, for in opening the door to your unconscious in this way, you are allowing your spouse to meet you at a special and unguarded place, the place of magic, often beyond common sense or even words. Whether or not your dreams make perfect sense to you or your partner (and you don't have to be Sigmund Freud to receive at least some of their meanings), being given a view of your beloved through this mysterious looking glass is to be taken into his or her spiritual privacy.

The same is true of the dreams that are aspirations—for in revealing our hopes and longings we are at once most exalted and most vulnerable. For in speaking of what we desire we also reveal how we can be disappointed. The fact that you always wanted to be a ballerina (and can't even walk across the living room without banging into the wall) is something you don't want everyone to know, but telling your sweetheart is a way of opening up a sensitive part of yourself for special nurturing.

None of us can live out all our dreams—life isn't long enough. And we all have more talents than time to explore them in. Although at some level we realize that, as my mother used to say, "You can't do everything," there is also a sense of loss attached to letting go of even our most ridiculous or offbeat dreams. When we share our unfulfilled dreams, we are asking our loved ones to meet us in a place of vulnerability, where we can be apprehended not only for who we are, but also for who we would like to have been.

Revealing your dreams is an act of trust. It means you believe that the person who loves you desires to see you in your secret essence without being horrified or ashamed, without making fun of you. It means you believe you can share your innermost secrets, and that if your aspirations should turn to ashes, the person you love will still be there to comfort you.

Be Generous with Your Body

True love needs the foundation of physical affection. Bodies not only house our spirits, they express our spirits. They communicate, without words, the essence of our beings.

When we were babies, we received the feeling of being loved through the sensations we felt in the presence of our parents' bodies. Being nestled next to your mother's heart, being lifted up and carried in your father's strong arms—these were the physical sensations that gave us a sense of security and made us feel loved.

If you received the blessings of physical kindness and attention from your parents, these are feelings you wish to return to, and if you never received such tender nurturance and affection, this is a state you long to finally arrive at.

When our bodies are joyous, our emotions are positive and our spirits are uplifted. Therefore, the gift of your beloved's body, more than anything else, can make you feel loved. As Peter said, "After I make love to you I feel as if anything is possible."

So be generous with your body, and not only when you are making love. Give each other a foot massage or a back rub. Prepare a cool washcloth for a fevered brow, or a mud pack for a bee sting. Wrap an ace bandage around a sprained ankle. Be the bearer of Band-Aids, soup, and medicines.

Kiss for no reason; allow your warmhearted hug of greeting to become a deep embrace. Let your hand brush the shoulder of your beloved when you pass by her in the kitchen. Touch his wooly arm when you sit beside him on the couch. Let the curve of her foot make your foot less lonely while you fall asleep. When he's broken-hearted, touch his face; when she is discouraged, hold her head like a precious bowl between your two hands.

Let your bodies speak your truth. Make love with the consciousness that your body can say what you cannot, and know that in its sensuous abandon sexual passion is the dancing of the spirit.

TRUST ONE ANOTHER

True love is built upon trust, the emotional climate you jointly create as the atmosphere in which love can flourish. Trust is the sense that we are safe with one another, that in our moments of vulnerability, weakness, or great glory, we will not be betrayed.

To trust means that we start from the position of believing that our sweetheart is motivated by a deep concern for us, that he or she, in spite of occasional missteps or mistakes, truly has our well-being in mind. When we trust, we believe that the other loves us dearly and intends to love us well and long. Trust imagines the best; trust expects the happiest possible outcome. Trust serves with joy in the expectation that trust will be returned.

Trust develops trust. Acknowledging that you trust the person you love—with your life, with your heart, your body, your talents, your fears, your children, your worldly goods—invites him or her to become even more worthy of that trust. In a wonderful upward spiral, the compliment of trust encourages even more trustworthiness. Thus the more you trust, the safer you become and the more you are able to love.

Just as trust engenders trust, doubt, its opposite, creates more suspicion. The more you suspect, expect, and imagine that your partner doesn't love you and doesn't want to care for you properly, the more it will become impossible for him or her to scale the wall of your doubt to give you the gift of love, the blessing of undying affection.

But trust comes from more than your own state of mind. It develops in response to the actions, words, and ways of the person you are choosing to trust. Trust is delicate, easily damaged; it can be destroyed by a single sentence of spirit-crushing attack, one thoughtless night of betrayal, a passel of lies. In matters of trust, we are the guardians of one another's psyches—and we must take the creation of trust as a serious responsibility.

Therefore, as well as trusting, be trustworthy yourself. Ask the best of yourself—for integrity with your actions, intentions, and words—so you may be a worthy partner in creating the atmosphere of trust that will be a lifetime cradle for your love.

DO IT AGAIN AND AGAIN AND AGAIN

There's a gypsy I know who will read your palm, and answer any two questions for ten dollars. If there's anything amiss in your life, a wish that's hard to make true, she always asks for a hundred dollars so she can burn ten candles for ten days and light your wish into reality.

I've always wondered whether she really burns the candles or if it's just a hype for more money. But either way, she has a point: wishes don't come true by wishing them once. They become actualized through effort and attention; and just as the gypsy lights the candles to insure results, it's holding the flame of desire in our hearts and minds, in our emotions and actions, that will bring our most heart-felt wishes into being.

Behavior is difficult to change. It takes practice and repetition. This is no less true about the behaviors of love. Learning to think differently about the person you love and incorporating new emotional behaviors is a process that takes time. You won't learn the actions of love in a minute, nor will they become your possession simply by reading this book. You will have to remember them and act them out over and over again in order to get permanent results.

The behaviors of love affect us like nourishment: when we're hungry, we eat and are satisfied. But that doesn't mean we won't be hungry again, won't need again to be filled. Just because once we remembered to kindle the romance or to acknowledge the hardships our circumstances create, doesn't mean that we've done it for all time. We all need the benedictions and courtesies of love over and over again. None of us has been so blessed and indulged that we don't need all the good things we can possibly get.

Like a wish or a work of art, the beauty of a relationship is sculpted over time. The love you imagine and desire will become yours only through a constancy of effort. So do all these things over and over again, and your relationship will flourish far and beyond your happiest imaginings.

THE
TRANSFORMATIONS
OF LOVE

CONSOLE ONE ANOTHER

More, perhaps, than we would like to acknowledge, life is infused with tragedy. Everybody is given burdens of heart that are almost too much to bear; we all have sorrows and heartaches that bring us into landscapes of pain which at times seem untraversable. There are times when we feel that what we are experiencing will utterly devour or destroy us.

To be aware of this is to know how immense is the need for consolation. Faced with the magnitude of the tragic in our midst, we can do nothing but attempt to extend the healing gift even if we feel totally unequipped to offer it. For no matter how inadequate the gesture may seem, it will reach into the place that is aching for solace.

Consolation is a spiritual undertaking. It begins with the state of grace that accepts we are all suffering and that it is one of our highest callings to move into the vale of tears with one another.

We all need to be willing to act as physicians of the spirit for one another during the painful times. For it is when we are assaulted by the visitation of life's sorrows that we most need to feel the presence of the person who loves us. It is when we are broken-hearted that we most need to be ministered to, when we are in grief that we need most to be taken into the arms of love.

Consoling is being willing to enter at the depth of the wound.

To console is to join company with, to bond. It is to enter into another's sorrow and stand in its presence, to become witness to the unbearable so that, finally, it can be borne.

To console is to comfort—with words, with your hands, with your heart, with your prayers. To console is to mourn with one another and thereby divide the power of the loss. In consoling you make yourself and the person you love less alone. You listen from the innermost place in yourself to the innermost place in her soul, respond from the most generous part of yourself to the neediest part of him.

FORGIVE ONE ANOTHER

To forgive is to see the person who has offended you in an entirely different way, through the eyes of charity and love. This is a difficult, but life-transforming task, for forgiveness breathes new life into a relationship and changes the chemistry between you from stale to sweet.

In a real sense, forgiveness begins with yourself, with the understanding that despite your best intentions, you too will fail, will find yourself doing the terrible things you thought only your enemies were capable of doing. To see yourself with compassion in spite of your failures is the beginning of forgiveness for others. For we can never take back into our hearts the person who has wounded us unless we can first be kind to ourselves about our own offenses.

Forgiveness requires emotional maturity and a willingness to move yourself into the future. To forgive is to start over, in a different place, to behave from the depths of your heart as if the bad thing never happened. In this sense forgiveness is a creative act; for it asks that you create a new relationship. Starting now.

This requires a deep internal transformation. Forgiveness is not forgetting—papering over the words or actions that wounded you. Rather, it is being willing to expand your heart so much that you can look at the wounding thing from a different, elevated perspective. To lift yourself up from the good guy/bad guy view of life to the place from which you can realize that we are all trying as hard as we can, but we are all flawed. We all partake of the imperfections of the human condition and we all have done or will do terrible, unforgivable things to one another.

Forgiveness asks that you see the person in the totality of his or her being, that you embrace your beloved in the whole range of his or her essence, understanding why he or she has done the wounding thing. Instead of remembering forever the petty crimes, insults, and abuses of the other person (and positing a future based on past disappointments and failures), forgiveness allow them to dissolve in the light of constantly renewing perception. In this sense forgiveness invites you to start over, remembering again the good that was there all along, allowing the bad things to blow away like milkweed floss in the wind.

ACKNOWLEDGE THE POWER
OF LANGUAGE TO CREATE REALITY

Language is a very powerful instrument. What we utter is what we believe or expect, and if we say it enough, in time what we speak becomes true. What we say, and what we hear others say, has the power to sculpt our experience, our view of the world, and perhaps most important, our view of ourselves. One of the great gifts of love is that, in its midst, we can marshal this powerful capability and use it to bring life, enlightenment, and healing to the person we most adore.

One form of emotional healing comes from the precise use of language—words you speak, and words that are spoken to you. Because of this, an intimate relationship and the verbal exchange intrinsic to it, have a greater capacity than almost anything else in the world to heal us of deep emotional wounds.

Words spoken to us by our loved ones truly have the capacity to heal our memories and deeply imprinted pains, and to recreate our sense of ourselves and of the world. This means that the negative words which shaped your early consciousness and/or your perception of yourself—"You're ugly"; "You can't have that; we're too poor"; "You never pay attention"; "Why can't you keep your mouth shut?" can actually be revised, corrected, and dispelled through the careful use of language.

Scott had been endlessly yelled at for how he had behaved at school, told what a mess he made of his school books, punished for being late, and criticized for getting C's. Nobody had ever bothered to note his intuitive genius, the extraordinary function of his mind. Years of ravaged self-esteem began to be healed for Scott the day his sweetheart first told him he was intelligent. "You're brilliant," she said, "I just love the way your mind works." "The minute she said that something inside me started to shift," he told me later. "I began to believe I wasn't stupid. The more she said it, the more I was able to believe her. And the more she said it, the more I noticed that other people sometimes said similar things. In time her words changed how I felt about myself entirely."

Language does have the power to change reality. Therefore, treat your words as the mighty instruments they are—to heal, to bring into being, to remove, as if by magic, the terrible violations of childhood, to nurture, to cherish, to bless, to forgive—to create from the whole cloth of your soul, TRUE LOVE.

Sanctify Your Relationship

Whether it is clearly visible or not, every relationship has a higher purpose than itself alone, a meaning that goes beyond the conventions of love and romance, and attaches the two people in it to a destiny that has roots in the past and wings in the future. This purpose is to shape us individually into the highest and best versions of ourselves, and to change, if only in some tiny way, the essential character of the reality we have entered here by being born.

To know this is to believe that whatever occurs between you— the petty dramas and traumas, the life-shaping tragedies—is honing you for your unique participation in the human stream. It is to accept that the person you love has come into your life for a reason that goes beyond the satisfactions of the moment or even your personal future to reach into the web of time beyond time.

What you do here together, how well and how beautifully you do it, has implications not only for how cozily you sit together in your rocking chairs in your old age, but also for every other living being. We are all participants in the process of creating a species and a world that hums with peace and is informed by love. This is our highest heritage, and when we sanctify our relationships, the difficulties and insults they contain will be instantly diminished and what will stand in their place is the overwhelming presence of real love.

Sanctifying your relationship means seeing it not as an act of self-indulgence, but as an offering of love that you deliver up with joy to the fulfillment of its higher meaning.

This entails not only an attitude of acceptance but also two behaviors: making speech and keeping silence. It means verbally acknowledging this higher truth to one another: "Thank you for being the instrument for the discovery of my purpose"; "I know we have come together for an important reason"; " I love you for being my way to see the holiness of life."

At times it also means keeping the silence in your heart which is a thanksgiving of this higher purpose, or engaging together in a practice meditation which is a walking together in spirit, a prayer that your purpose together be revealed.

Your love is a stitch in the fabric of the All. To see it as such is to place your relationship in the ultimate perspective and to receive from it the ultimate joy.

CONSECRATE YOUR RELATIONSHIP

We all need the paths of our lives to be marked out so that we can be reminded of the quality of our lives and the beauty of our loves. We dignify and consecrate our relationships when we set them apart from the ordinary through ritual. Personal rituals provide a reference not only for the value we place upon our relationships, but also for the value we ask be conferred upon them.

When I was a child, my father would always say a prayer before dinner on my birthday: "With thanksgiving and love that you have been given to be a part of our hearts and of our family, we celebrate this day of your birth, beautiful child, delightful spirit. May you have a year full of joy and may your prodigious talents, like arrows, find their true mark through a long life in this world."

In the presence of these consecrating words, my life became more than simply the life I was leading. It became a holy place, with qualities and possibilities. It became a privilege and a responsibility. No matter what difficult times I came to, no matter what hardships I faced, the ritual of these consecrated words was a beautiful reference that pointed me to my higher purpose.

Relationships, also, should be consecrated in this way, made holy by the rituals and ceremonies that, in their mystical capacity, have the power to set them apart. Ceremonies say, in effect, this day is not like all other days, this person is not like all other people; this love is not like all other loves. Not only in our hearts but also in our actions, we intend it to be a union of meaning, with allegiance to a lofty mission.

While we may think of consecration as something that can only happen in a church, we all have the capacity to hallow our relationships. The consecration of your relationship is a creative and deeply private affair. Set aside a special time to acknowledge your union—your wedding anniversary perhaps; designate a specific place in which to honor it; and create your own private ceremony—light candles, say words, play music.

Consecrating your relationship is the sign, repeated and beautiful, that you choose to view your relationship as holy, as no mistake, and that you intend, through it and with your beloved as your witness, always to live it to the highest of its purpose.

Hold Each Other in the Light

A relationship is always far more than we imagine or expect it to be. It is more than a living arrangement, more than being together in a social circumstance, more than the bright-colored kite tail of romance; it is the coming together of two persons whose spirits participate with one another, beautifully and painfully, in the inexorable process of their individual becoming.

In this respect, relationships are like relentless grinding stones, polishing and refining us to the highest level of our radiance. It is this radiance that is the highest expression of love—this is why a relationship is a spiritual enterprise.

When we look at the person we love with the expectation that he or she will or should solve all our emotional problems or make all our worldly dreams come true, we reduce that person to a pawn in our own self-serving plot, seeing the relationship as an experience of *what can I get,* rather than *what can I become?*

When we view a relationship from a different vantage point—one that acknowledges it as a spiritual incubator—we come to see the person we love differently. We see him or her as separate from our hopes, from our demands that he or she be a particular way right now, for us. Rather, we recognize our sweetheart as a spiritual accomplice; we hold our beloved in the light.

Holding your love in the light is seeing the other as a soul in a constant state of becoming, encountering your beloved in all the radiance of his or her own being and strivings-to-be. To hold the other in the light is to seek the pure spirit that lies behind the limitations of individual psychology and social circumstance, to apprehend the full essence of your beloved, as she was since time began, as he shall be for all time after.

To do this is to reach beyond the petty and even gigantic disappointments that you experience in making your life together to apprehend the divinity of this single unique and exquisite being who has been given to join you on the journey of your own becoming.

To hold each other in the light is to see one another as God would see you, perfectly engaged in the process of becoming perfect.

BOW TO THE MYSTERY OF LOVE

A relationship—two people coming together to live, to work, to play, to laugh, to grieve, to rejoice, to make love—is the form that human beings give to love, but love itself, that ineffable essence that draws us together into communion with one another, is beyond definition, beyond analysis. Love has its own way. Love just Is.

Love is a mystery, the essence of which is angelic. In its very nature it goes beyond what we can understand by any of the systems through which we usually comprehend reality. It exists simultaneously outside us and within us. It both binds and frees us. It opens our hearts and breaks our hearts. It cannot be seen, except in the eyes of the beloved, nor felt except in the heart of the one who is cherished. Invisible, its absence leaves us gray-hearted, wounded in spirit, while its presence transforms our hearts, our psyches, and our lives.

We seek love, without knowing what it is, knowing we will know when we find it. This is the true mystery of love—that no matter how much we are unable to describe it, we always recognize it when we experience it.

Love infuses itself into relationships by means that are beyond our invention or imagining. Sometimes love comes to stay, nourished and coddled by the feelings and efforts of those who have invited it in. But if it is not honored or nurtured, love will go off to seek its true home.

In bowing to the mystery of love we acknowledge that love is beyond our comprehension, that we will never fully understand it. The love we seek seeks us, embraces us without our knowing, and binds our spirits into the body of itself. There is a point at which in the presence of love there is nothing more to say or prove, nothing left to ask for or regret, nothing left except the miracle of love itself.

ABOUT THE AUTHOR

For more than twenty-five years, Daphne Rose Kingma has worked as a psychotherapist helping thousands of individuals and couples understand and improve their relationships. Dubbed the "Love Doctor" by the *San Francisco Chronicle*, Daphne has appeared as a relationship expert on nationally broadcast television programs including *Oprah!*, *Sally Jessy Raphael*, and *The Leeza Gibbons Show*. The best-selling author of several books, including *Coming Apart*, *The Book of Love*, *365 Days of Love*, *The Nine Types of Lovers*, and *Weddings from the Heart*, she lives in Denver, Colorado.

To find out more about Daphne, visit her website at
www.daphnekingma.com

Conari Press publishes books on topics ranging from spirituality, personal growth, and relationships to women's issues, parenting, and social issues. Our mission is to publish quality books that will make a difference in people's lives—how we feel about ourselves and how we relate to one another. We value integrity, compassion, and receptivity, both in the books we publish and in the way we do business.

As a member of the community, we dedicate a portion of our proceeds from certain books to charitable causes and continually look for new ways to use natural resources as wisely as possible.

Our readers are our most important resource, and we value your input, suggestions, and ideas about what you would like to see published. Please feel free to contact us, to request our latest book catalog, or to be added to our mailing list.

Conari Press
An imprint of Red Wheel/Weiser, LLC
P.O. Box 612
York Beach, ME
03910-0612
800-423-7087
www.conari.com